COUTURE

GRAPHIQUE

AUTHORS
JOS ARTS
ELS DE BAAN
NANDA VAN DEN BERG
TAMSIN BLANCHARD
ANDREA KRISTIĆ
MARCO PECORARI
MARIJ RYNJA
JOSÉ TEUNISSEN
HANKA VAN DER VOET

GRAPHIQUE

COUTURE

FASHION, GRAPHIC DESIGN & THE BODY

EDITED BY JOSÉ TEUNISSEN, HANKA VAN DER VOET & JAN BRAND

TERRA

MOTI

CONTENTS

Katharine Hamnett, *Ocean Project* for the British department store Selfridges, 2011

PREFACE –
TWO DISCIPLINES CONVERGE

— MIEKE GERRITZEN

In the past century, fashion has undergone so many artistic developments and broadened its scope to such an extent that it has become an integral part of our visual culture. Meanwhile, production in low-wage countries has reduced the price of clothing considerably and put fashion within almost everyone's reach. As a result, the fashion industry has grown to be one of the biggest sectors within the West's consumer-oriented society, and clothing has almost become a disposable good that is purchased — often online — on a weekly basis.

In this book, curator and lecturer José Teunissen demonstrates how the fashion industry is changing, and how it has found itself at the intersection of several different disciplines. She puts the contemporary fashion world in context by examining its evolution from both a fashion design and a graphic design perspective and demonstrates how these two disciplines are converging. Clothing determines a person's identity at the same time as communicating his or her attitudes and behaviour, and graphic design in fashion is playing an ever greater role in conveying that identity. Similarly, branding, marketing and increasingly 'new' media have become ever more important as ways of communicating this message. There is absolutely no doubt that fashion is on its way to becoming one of the most influential players in the development of the creative sector.

Thanks to our media-based lifestyles, a person is now confronted with more images every day than someone in medieval times would have seen in an entire lifetime, and fashion makes a considerable contribution to this huge flow of images. The pace of change within the fashion industry can be compared to the transience of social media: the fact that people enjoy sharing information and being part of a community is nothing new for the fashion sector, especially among young people. It is all about the fashion brand; you only 'belong' if you are wearing the 'right' one. Take the T-shirt, for example. It has long fulfilled the role of a pamphlet, a vehicle for quick quotes, slogans or statements, and these developments have gone hand in hand with prestigious couture houses developing their own unique visual identities.

Over the decades, a steadfast yet imaginative approach to their visual identities has been key to the successes of many of the major fashion houses: Louis Vuitton, Hermès and Paul Smith for example. It is here, that the two professions, fashion and graphic design, converge and become visible, literally. The use of graphic elements is not restricted to clothing, but can also be seen in accessories, printed materials, digital media and films.

In this book, Teunissen illustrates how graphic art plays an important part in fashion's rich visual culture and demonstrates how it has become deeply rooted in art and fashion history. People have been using decorative patterns to add character to their clothing for centuries. Although mainly for aesthetic reasons in the past, graphics are now often adopted to fulfil both an aesthetic and an informative/communicative role. The patterns on clothes, the rhythm of textures, light-sensitive fabrics... these are just some of the latest expressive platforms being explored within fashion colleges around the world, but the real challenge is to find the right balance between aesthetic and informative quality.

Just as in other industries, digitalisation is stimulating innovation in fashion and allowing the general public to become more actively involved. While the designers should in theory be the ones to develop new 'information decorations' for garments, new tools continue to emerge which enable fashion-conscious consumers to determine the appearance of their own clothing. It may soon be possible to pre-programme the colours and patterns for knitwear, for example, to produce garments featuring one's own images or designs.

Couture Graphique shows us that clothing in the twenty-first century forms an integral part of our complex, media-based society. Not only fashion but also other disciplines such as graphic design are on the verge of change. The convergence of fashion, design and media makes way for new links between broader social issues such as the social structure of communication, sustainability and economic growth.

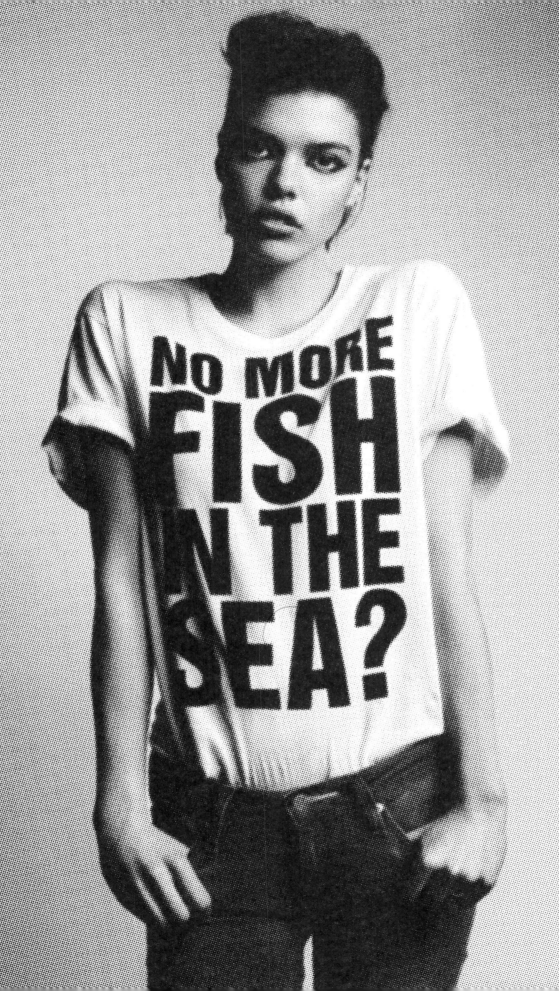

Katharine Hamnett, *Ocean Project* for the British department store Selfridges, 2011

Erté alphabet, 1927

INTRODUCTION

— JOSÉ TEUNISSEN

Fashion designers always work in teams, with an army of dressmakers, seamstresses and assistant designers behind them in the studio lending body and shape to their fashion house or label. But since the Eighties, all major fashion companies have also had an art director in charge of creating special invitations, lookbooks, packaging, advertising campaigns and store design. That development marked a turning point for fashion houses; it was when they shifted their focus from the garments themselves to a 'total look' — a clear, overarching visual style to emphasise the designer's image and signature. This development is examined in more detail by Tamsin Blanchard and Marco Pecorari.

Small, conceptual avant-garde brands such as Comme des Garçons, Yohji Yamamoto and Martin Margiela pioneered this trend, but by the end of the Nineties traditional couture houses were following in their footsteps and making large-scale changes. The first step was often to recruit young fashion designers to breathe new life into the floundering world of *haute couture* with spectacular, experimental collections. Alexander McQueen and John Galliano succeeded in putting Givenchy and Dior back on the map, boosting their appeal to a larger, and younger, audience. This was rapidly followed by the arrival of new art directors to 'modernise' the brand's visual image. They too were tasked with broadening the appeal of the fashion house — which until that time had really been focused on a small group of older elite who could afford such luxury items — to include a larger, younger audience. In the Nineties, classic coat and jacket brand Burberry employed art director Christopher Bailey to carry out a rebranding exercise without changing the products themselves. He used advertorials and advertising campaigns to create a completely new and updated image for the brand. In 1997, luxury luggage brand Louis Vuitton appointed Marc Jacobs to develop a coordinating clothing collection, although this only caught on when he enlisted the help of graffiti artist Stephen Sprouse in 2000; Sprouse revamped the LV monogram by spraying it graffiti-style on a Speedy Bag. It was the start of a long-running experiment in which the classic logo would be captured by a series of different artists in monograms that retained the unmistakable look of Louis Vuitton, yet were consistently new and innovative. A combination of heritage — part of the brand's appeal is linked to its long history as a mark of quality — and modern visual language introduced by the artists through graffiti and other visual techniques, have transformed Louis Vuitton into one of the most popular brands of the twenty-first century. In *Marc & the Monogram*, Nanda van den Berg details how the logo has evolved in the past decade. Since 2011, Louis Vuitton has dedicated a section of its stores to art and artists, something which other fashion houses have also adopted. Similarly, over the last ten years, we have seen luxury brands incorporating an increasing number of different disciplines (in terms of both architecture and design). Nowadays, graphic design, architecture, store design, websites and most recently even films, all contribute to a brand's total look.

Louis Vuitton, *Speedy Bag*, 1997

FASHION & COMMUNICATION

Fashion is not (and in fact has never been) merely about decorating the body. Fashion and clothing offer ways for us to communicate with one another every day. We express who we are by making our bodies 'readable'. While the difference between clothes and fashion lies in the smallest details, it is notable that the graphic element has continued to gain influence throughout the decades. Sonia Delaunay, for instance, began her surrealistic period with a *Robe Poème* (1923): a dress with a verse on it. In the years that followed, however, clothes in the fashion world remained text-free. As far as we know, American universities' sports garments were the first items of clothing to have text — the college logo — printed on them.

All that changed in the late Fifties when the T-shirt, hitherto worn as an undergarment, made the transition to outerwear, teamed with a pair of jeans. In the youth culture of the Sixties, the T-shirt proved the ideal medium for expressing one's political ideology. The use of the T-shirt to make a statement became even more pronounced during the Seventies' punk movement. Spotting this garment's potential, designers such as Vivienne Westwood/Malcolm McLaren (1977) and later Katharine Hamnett (1983) placed it at the forefront of their collections. Today, the T-shirt (whether with logo, image or text) still remains crucial to many cult streetwear brands such as KAWS and Piet Parra. Furthermore, for sportswear brands it is the key garment (along with sports shoes) for expressing the overall identity of the brand and/or football club. As illustrated in *Inscribing the body* by Hanka van der Voet and José Teunissen, the T-shirt has become a vehicle for displaying a brand's identity, image and creativity.

Vivienne Westwood, *Destroy T-shirt*, 1977

FROM LABEL TO TOTAL LOOK

The arrival of the label signalled the entry of graphic design into fashion. In 1858, tailor Charles Frederick Worth opened a fashion house and started designing and selling his own couture. The labels sewn in, like an artist's signature, marked the start of fashion as a form of creative expression. As a result, fashion designers were soon developing their own styles both with their clothing designs and through the typography on their labels, the packaging for perfumes and accessories.

With *Chanel No. 5* in 1921, Coco Chanel was the first to create a contemporary, yet timeless visual style which was beautifully echoed in her fashion collections. By repeatedly drawing on a repertoire of distinctive elements: contrasting trim, the interlocking letters 'C' on the Chanel buttons, the string of pearls, the camellia and the bag with chain, she managed to develop an unmistakable, graphic look which forms the starting point for Karl Lagerfeld's collections even to this day. In other words, Chanel was the first fashion brand with a coherent, clearly recognisable visual style.

Since the Eighties, almost all fashion brands have placed art directors in charge of developing a clear visual style. The result has been not only recognisable brands, but also a broader visual identity comprising leaflets, lookbooks and special invitations. With his company Aboud Sodano, Alan Aboud devised the image for the Paul Smith label in 1989. It consisted of a multi-coloured stripe combined with the words 'Paul Smith' in a hand-written font. These two elements, which feature on all products, packaging and invitations, continue to define the Paul Smith brand with its mix of classic English style and Sixties' Carnaby Street colours. In *From label to total look*, José Teunissen looks at a brand's visual language in more detail.

Paul Smith, *Multi-colour logo*, 1989

From 1990 onwards, Paul Boudens collaborated with Walter Van Beirendonck and also developed invitations and lookbooks for Haider Ackermann and Yohji Yamamoto. For a time, Bernhard Willhelm gave the Dutch photography duo Carmen Freundenthal and Elle Verhagen free rein to create unique catalogues. What did the art directors bring to the fashion brands, and how has fashion changed over the years? Marco Pecorari answers that question in his *'Zones-in between': the ontology of a fashion praxis*.

FASHION AS GRAPHIC DESIGN

In 1913, during her Futurism period, Sonia Delaunay designed the 'simultaneous dress'. Using contrasting patches of fabric, she intended to illustrate the contemporary relationship with time — the fragmentation of time and space. It was an adaptation to modern life. Of Walter Van Beirendonck, one could say that he is a modern-day designer who carries out graphic experiments on bodies. Van Beirendonck says he draws inspiration from art, literature and ethnic influences and his work is typified by bold, graphic patterns with an almost comic-book feel with which he creates his own universe. His manner of working has since been picked up and adapted by younger designers such as Bernhard Willhelm, Henrik Vibskov and Bas Kosters. Notably, Vibskov and Kosters work not only as fashion designers, but also as musicians and artists. In the universes they create, various disciplines have merged, as illustrated by Els de Baan in *Fashion & graphic design: idiosyncratic visual language as a total concept*.

Sonia Delaunay, *Simultaneous dress*, 1913

THE FASHION FILM & OTHER INNOVATIVE TECHNOLOGICAL INFLUENCES

In recent years, the fashion film has become increasingly popular as a new medium for supporting designers' brands. Former photographers and graphic designers regularly work on short films that are intended to promote a brand's new collection or concept (and/or attract visitors to the website).

The growth of broadband internet and social media has had a tremendous impact on the opportunities for visual marketing, and in order to maximise one's reach among a young audience, it is essential to communicate online. Hanka van der Voet outlines the many possibilities films and websites present in *Fashion & film: a power shift*. As far as these new media are concerned, it is still an 'emerging market'. Renowned photographers such as Nick Knight and Van Lamsweerde/Matadin as well as relative newcomers like Zach Gold playing an influential part in its development. If we are looking for the answer to how the fashion film will affect the further development of a brand's visual image, we are just going to have to wait and see.

According to Hanka van der Voet and José Teunissen in *Fashion, technology & the smartphone*, the latest technological innovations are also changing the way we view the body. Designers such as Issey Miyake, Junya Watanabe, Hussein Chalayan, Iris van Herpen, Pauline van Dongen and Simon Thorogood are utilising new technologies and materials to explore the physical and psychological relationships we have with the world around us. These designers are driven by a fascination for new materials themselves, and are using new techniques to discover fresh new shapes. To them, the body is merely a medium for expressing their ideas about corporality, sexuality and the future. Fashion is no longer about creating the 'fashionable woman' or communicating one's identity, but rather the body and what you clothe it in has become the ideal vehicle for illustrating a person's experience of the body, of space and time in the context of the virtual world that is now playing an ever greater role in our daily lives.

Hussein Chalayan, *Geotropics*, S/S 1992

Iris van Herpen, MICRO haute couture, S/S 2012

FROM LABEL TO TOTAL LOOK: THE VARIOUS ROUTES TO A BRAND IDENTITY

— JOSÉ TEUNISSEN

Nowadays, it is hard to find clothing that does not have a brand name; it might be just a subtle label inside a garment or a minuscule Nike tag on a T-shirt, or it could be an all-over monogram print like those seen on Louis Vuitton bags. Brand names can even be found on underwear, socks, packaging and wrapping paper. Whether a brand, a monogram or a tag, they permeate entire stores, right down to the sales receipts.

We rarely stop to think that these brands are in direct contact with our bodies and that we are in fact acting as living, breathing billboards. "The brand is a symbol that is soaked with a special kind of power, set somewhere in between language, commodity and their respective values. Brands do not only serve to distinguish one product from another; they are the embodiment of a concept, a value, an emotion and a story," says Patricia Calefato.[1] While a brand can be seen as a mark of the price/quality ratio of the clothing itself, its role in communicating the philosophy and values of the fashion house behind it is more important: Chanel exudes timeless, classic chic; Hermès expresses a yearning for perfect and ultimate quality; while the wearer of Comme des Garçons gains an air of quirkiness and avant-garde taste.

This brings us to a striking paradox. While the wearers believe that their clothing helps to shape and reflect their individual identity, they are actually communicating the identity of a brand. So what exactly is the role of the logo and the brand name in contemporary fashion? How and when did this logo mania develop, and how have various fashion brands created their own visual languages and communication styles?

ORIGINS OF THE LABEL

In 1858 Charles Frederick Worth opened a fashion house selling ready-to-wear sample designs in Paris, and shortly afterwards created his own label. Until then, there had been a *couture à façon* in which tailors developed new dresses to the bidding of well-heeled ladies. So when Worth introduced his seasonal ranges of off-the-peg dresses, haute couture — the practice of made-to-measure dressmaking with the creator at the helm — was born. This new

1 Patricia Calefato, 'Taal en Mode. Van naam van God naar de macht van het merk', in: *Mode en Verbeelding*. ArtEZ press/d' jonge Hond, Arnhem 2009, p 128.

approach transformed fashion into an art form: from now on, garments would be conceived and designed by creative minds, 'couturiers', who just like artists soon started leaving their signatures on their creations, albeit in the form of sewn-in labels. The label 'Worth, 7 Rue de la Paix, Paris' was used from 1860 onwards in response to the trade of illegal copies of Worth's creations. At the same time as this adoption of the maker's label, the use of brand names was on the rise. "It is surely no accident that the development of the couture label in the second half of the nineteenth century coincided with a growing commercial emphasis on brand names, especially in the burgeoning field of advertising, where it was widely recognized that profits could be made by linking a desirable commodity with a particular brand name," states Nancy Troy.[2]

The Paquin and Jeanne Lanvin fashion houses, along with Paul Poiret a little later, followed in Worth's footsteps and started sewing labels bearing their name into their creations. Each designer developed a distinct graphic style which they also carried through to perfume bottles and packaging.

CHANEL AS A TOTAL LOOK

The first designer to develop a coherent visual style (that which we now call a brand image) was Coco Chanel in the early Twenties. She introduced a visual style, as seen in her *Chanel No. 5* perfume (1921) for example, which was reflected elegantly in designs for her clothing and accessories. By building up a repertoire of recurring details in the twentieth century, such as the contrasting trim, the interlinked 'CC' on the Chanel button, the string of pearls, the camellia and the bag with the chain, Coco Chanel managed to create a visual style that was so distinct that it continues to form the basis for Karl Lagerfeld's Chanel collections today.[3]

Compared to her contemporaries such as Paul Poiret and Jeanne Lanvin, Chanel was revolutionary in the way she introduced fabrics and garments from the worlds of sport and menswear: jerseys; the beret; the cardigan; trousers, into women's fashion, making it more functional. Women had been forced to go out to work during the First World War and they were not about to relinquish their new-found independence. As it became more widely accepted for women to have jobs and go out on their own, women's clothing needed to change and needed to become more practical. Chanel was the first designer to also consider comfort: pockets were incorporated into clothing and she designed a handbag for carrying money and keys in. Excessive amounts of fabric, embroidery and lace were replaced with comfortable jumpers and knitwear.

In the Twenties, when it was still considered normal for a woman to show off her husband's wealth through her lavishly decorated garments made from luxurious fabrics, Chanel's restrained chic was called, scathingly, the 'poverty look'. Nevertheless, Chanel soon became successful with her knitted suits and *La Petite Robe Noire* (the little black dress, 1924) because it symbolised emancipation: women could work comfortably in her garments without having to get changed five times a day. In actual fact, the style of women's fashion became equally restrained, functional and timeless as men's fashion had in the nine-teenth century with the arrival of the men's suit. At that time, the suit also represented new values, those of an industrialising and democratising society in which the bourgeoisie was on the up and ideals of enlightenment were shaping individualism.[4]

2 Nancy Troy, *Couture Culture*, MIT, Cambridge 2003, pp. 25, 26.

3 Jean Marie Floch, 'Chanel changing: The total look', in: *Visual Identities*, pp. 85–115. The following clothing innovations are attributed to Chanel: marine blouse (1913), the jersey (1916), cardigans and knitted suits (1918), trousers (1920), the little black dress (1924), the blazer with gold buttons and the sailor's hat (1926), use of tweed (1928), costume jewellery (1930), the braid-edged tweed suit and the gold-chain belt (1956), the black-toed shoe and the quilted bag with gold chain (1957), and last but not least the bow in 1958. See Floch, p. 88.

4 See Anne Hollander, *Sex and Suit*. Albert Knopf, New York 1994, and Gilles Lipovetsky, *The Empire of Fashion: Fashion and Democracy*. Princeton University Press, Oxford 1994.

Louis Vuitton store in New York, decorated by Takashi Murakami, 2008

In the Twenties, Chanel also created a new feminine identity which expressed social change. Many of her inventions, remain classic outfits to this day. The distinctness of 'the timeless and classic' Chanel style is further enhanced by a series of sophisticated graphic additions: "In the drawing, we see a shoe with a black pointed toe, a padded bag with a golden chain, the famous little black dress, a multicoloured brooch shaped as a cross, the Chanel suit jacket, a bow, a camellia and, finally, the golden button embossed with the double C."[5] With this series of regular ingredients, Chanel constructed a 'fashion grid' that could be used as a simple guideline by all of the couturiers to follow her, from Gianfranco Ferré to Karl Lagerfeld, and Karl Lagerfeld still uses these basic elements when designing his new collections today. With her logos, buttons and graphic details, Chanel can be seen as the creator of the 'total look' far before the term had even been thought of, as well as the mind behind the fashion grid, a concept that would not be developed by other fashion houses until 'fashion branding' became a hot topic in the Eighties.[6]

THE FASHION HOUSE AS A BRAND

According to Floch, a fashion house's brand or total look is determined by concrete characteristics such as a silhouette, the lines, fabrics, light, the way accessories and clothing are combined, the use of colour and the way the body is presented. In Chanel's case, these features include a preference for monochrome colour combinations like black, white and beige, and silhouettes composed of understated, minimalistic, geometric sections which are decorated with 'baroque'-like details such as bracelets and sumptuous necklaces.[7] Even colourful tweed contrasts with the harsh lines of the suit. Floch concludes that by doing this, Chanel managed to create the female counterpart of the 'dandy': with its sober shapes, monochrome colours and graphic elements, the Chanel look can be compared to the men's suit. Then there are the carefully placed 'baroque' elements, perhaps better described as 'feminine' elements, that are added to the suits — of course only the Chanel suit could possibly be this colourful — and not to be forgotten, the elaborate necklaces and bracelets which interrupt the clean lines of the Chanel silhouette with even more 'baroqueness'. "All of these elements that cause any 'look' to be truly and fundamentally a visual identity are so many choices that proceed, in short, from a certain 'vision' of how a woman should dress," states Floch. "The phrase 'total look' emphasizes that it comes across as a closed unit and as a whole which is both perceptible and intelligible."[8]

LOGO MANIA

At the end of the Nineties, fashion houses Louis Vuitton and Gucci took a completely different approach to creating a fashion brand identity. Both names were originally manufacturers of luxury luggage and leather goods, and did not produce any clothing at all until the end of the twentieth century. After Moët et Chandon and Hennessy had merged, the new company acquired Louis Vuitton in 1987 to form Louis Vuitton, Moët, Hennessy (LVMH) as the world's largest luxury goods conglomerate, which would later include Givenchy too. When the classical fashion houses Givenchy and Dior embarked on a major renewal process in 1997, recruiting young designers such as Alexander McQueen and John

5 J. Marie Floch calls this the "spiritual patrimonium of Chanel", ibid. p. 86.

6 See the article by Tamsin Blanchard in this book.

7 This is fashion jewellery, i.e. replica jewels: these were also invented by Chanel, who thus not only emancipated but also democratised, since costume jewellery was accessible to a much larger group of women.

8 Floch, ibid. p. 92, 93.

Galliano to breathe new life into the struggling haute couture industry, Louis Vuitton immediately followed suit, bringing Marc Jacobs on board to develop a clothing line to match its range of bags. The brand enjoyed renewed popularity when, in 2000, the designer enlisted the help of graffiti artist Stephen Sprouse to revamp the logo for its bags; Sprouse restyled the traditional LV monogram by spray-painting a Speedy Bag. It marked the start of a long-running experiment in which various artists produced their own take on the classic logo, resulting in monograms that were new and refreshing, yet remained distinctly 'Louis Vuitton'. This combination of 'heritage' — the brand's appeal lies in its rich history and reputation for quality — and 'modern visual language', which artists inject with graffiti and other graphic techniques, has made Louis Vuitton one of the most popular fashion brands, with its bag becoming a firm favourite.

Just a few years earlier, in 1994, when the company was taken over by Investcorp, Gucci recruited Tom Ford as art director. Just like Jacobs, he was tasked with rejuvenating the company and bringing its visual image up to date by developing a new fashion line. He too was expected to open up the luxury brand to a wider and younger fashion audience, which up until then had been aimed at a small, older elite. Just as Louis Vuitton in the late Nineties, Gucci became immensely popular with its wide range of bags, which were all based on the original monogram (two overlapping letters 'G', dating from 1936) combined with a green-red stripe and bamboo handle. But Tom Ford could also allow himself the luxury of adding completely new details — something quite unique for classic brands due to the firmly held belief that to maintain its appeal a product needs to be distinctly recognisable, albeit with subtle variations. According to luxury brand specialist Bruno Remaury: "One must 'change without changing' avoiding sudden departures that might damage the clarity of the message."[9] Nevertheless, though Tom Ford's overhaul of Gucci was much more radical than the Louis Vuitton revamp, the brand's popularity did not suffer. An example of one particularly legendary Gucci campaign was the model's pubic hair shaved into the shape of the letter 'G'.

Classic luxury goods brands and fashion houses such as Gucci, Hermès, Chanel, Burberry and Louis Vuitton almost always refer to their heritage. "These logos/signs have progressively become a way of ensuring the continuity of the brand heritage they perpetuate, the emblem of brand (deformed, reworked, coloured), reminding consumers where the product comes from and at the same time serving as an identity symbol. In passing we must also mention that this type of heritage must be handled delicately, and in the same way that the evolution of a stylistic heritage must be 'iconoclastic', that of the emblematic heritage must be discreet," states Bruno Remaury.[10]

Jacques Derrida formulates the power of brands in general, as follows: "In order to function, that is, to be readable, a signature must have a repeatable, iterable, imitable form; it must be able to be detached from the present and singular intention of its productions. It is its sameness which, by corrupting its identity and its singularity, divides its seal (sceau)."[11] As a result of logo mania and widespread adoption of the monogram, the product itself loses importance, and everything (any products, perfumes, cosmetics) can be 'swallowed up' by the brand. The exterior of the Louis Vuitton store on New York's Fifth Avenue, for example, is completely covered by the LV emblem. This has turned the brand into an image (in this case a pattern) making it more about the graphic effect than the meaning.[12] And many fashion houses have become very skilled at this particular game.

9. Bruno Remaury, 'From the shop window to the museum: the relationship between a brand and its heritage', in: *Research report n 2*. IFM Paris, p. 21.

10 Bruno Remaury, ibid. p. 21.

11 Jacques Derrida, 'Signature Event Context' (1977), trans. Samuel Weber, in: Jacques Derrida, *Limited Inc*. Northwestern University Press, Evanston 1988.

12 Patricia Calefato, ibid. p. 128.

Gucci advertisement, photographed by Mario Testino, 2003

Viktor & Rolf, presentation of *Flowerbomb*, S/S 2005

Invitation for Viktor & Rolf by Piet Paris, S/S 2011

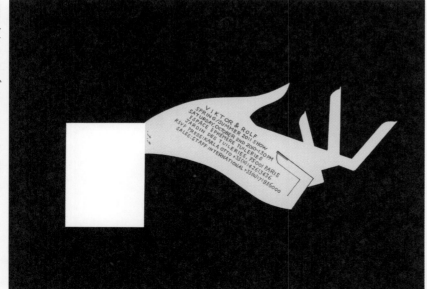

A BRAND'S FORM AND MESSAGE: VIKTOR & ROLF

13 Jay Hess, Simone Pasztorek, *Graphic Design for Fashion.* Laurence King Publishing, London 2010, p. 36.

14 'Mistreat' in the sense of shaving lines into fur coats or cutting holes in an evening dress.

The Viktor & Rolf monogram has followed a completely different, yet equally interesting path to becoming a brand. Dutch graphic designers Armand Mevis and Linda van Deursen designed the seal, featuring the letters V&R in relief and with raised edges just like a 'real wax seal', in 1999. "Fashion (and the language of fashion) works on a subconscious level. It appeals to the subconscious and because of that we probably (also subconsciously) made a connection with the surrealists, who tried to liberate imagination through hypnosis, dream analysis and so on," says Van Deursen. Mevis and Van Deursen were drawn to Salvador Dalí's soft watch as inspiration for the seal. While old-fashioned, the seal had no real function and was slightly out of proportion, and when used in black, it produced 'a posh, absurd fetish-like quality' that suited Viktor & Rolf. It is something you cannot really explain, but all those elements together worked for them.[13] The logo made its first appearance on the invitation for Viktor & Rolf's first *prêt-à-porter* show in 2000. Very satisfied with the seal, Viktor & Rolf subsequently used it on all their invitations, in their lookbooks and as the background to their catwalk shows. When the duo launched a men's fashion label some years later, they also gave the seal a prominent role in their collection and it was incorporated subtly into jackets, trousers and shirts. The seal was even featured on both the bottle and the packaging of their first perfume, *Flowerbomb 2005*, and it has been used in various ways in their accessories such as shoes, bags and glasses.

However, the seal is not the only element that makes Viktor & Rolf so recognisable. Just like Chanel, the duo's clothes play an important part in their visual language. Their repertoire predominantly comprises classical smart dress/occasion wear with recurring classics like the dinner jacket, the little black dress and the white shirt. Echoing Chanel once more, their designs also include a number of typical stylistic features. Viktor & Rolf often play around with proportions such as doubling the size of collars, or mistreating the clothes, acts which shatter the glamorous ideals of fashion and purposefully shock the onlooker.[14] Finally, Viktor & Rolf use an abundance of bows (like those used on the Dutch Princess Mabel's wedding dress), ruches (which can sometimes take on extreme proportions) and ribbons (as the packaging of their *Flowerbomb* perfume demonstrates).

A fashion brand works well when the shape of the label reflects the message, as Chanel beautifully illustrated. The same can be said of the Viktor & Rolf brand, but in a different way. After starting their label in 1993, the duo initially gained a reputation as conceptual fashion designers by presenting themselves and their criticism of the fashion world in performances and installations. They did not even waver from their conceptual image or their criticism of the industry when, in 2000, they received the financing they needed to launch as a commercial brand.

Viktor & Rolf worship the classic fashion dream and yearn for the glamour of yesteryear's haute couture. That yearning can be seen not only in their preference for classic designs such as the dinner jacket and the worlds they create at their shows, but also on their website which whisks visitors into a magical, black-and-white fashion palace. Just as the ruches and ribbons, the seal is a reflection of the same desire for a chic and classical image. Yet they also manage to distort and conceptualise these 'normal' elements: they designed a *Flowerbomb* collection (2006) for example, in which the 'creations' were made entirely out of ribbon, and they managed to add a playful touch to Princess

Viktor & Rolf logo by Mevis & Van Deursen

Mabel's wedding dress by arranging the bows in order of size from tiny to huge. In other words, Viktor & Rolf often take a conceptual approach to their collections, like they did when exploring the boundaries and significance of a piece of ribbon or a collar, as in *Flowerbomb 2006* and *Shirtsymphony 2011*. One could say then, that the seal represents this very combination of glamorous ideals which are slightly peculiar in their execution, and that like to explore the boundaries of fashion.

THE FASHION BRAND & NATIONAL IDENTITY: PAUL SMITH AND 'BRITISHNESS'

Paul Smith, known for his fourteen-colour pinstripe pattern, that up until recently influenced all his product lines from socks, perfumes and bags to the lining in his jackets, took a different approach to developing his label's brand identity. Paul Smith opened his first shop in 1970 and found international fame in the Eighties with the range of menswear that he presented in Paris. His logo and the distinct stripe did not make an appearance until 1989 when Paul Smith met graphic designer Alan Aboud. With his company Aboud Sodano, Aboud soon developed the handwritten 'Paul Smith' name for the label, with the stripes following a little later. These two elements would subsequently be used on all products, packaging materials and invitations, and came to define the Paul Smith brand, which was a mix of classic British tailoring and the colourful men's fashion found on Carnaby Street in the Sixties. Consumers who wear Paul Smith choose for: "Sensibility first and his clothing second," states Alice Goodrum in *The National Fabric*.[15] In her book, she outlines how a number of British fashion brands, including Paul Smith, globalised in the Nineties and became successful on the international stage, with Japan becoming a particularly important export market. In that context, it suddenly became necessary for a brand to not only be recognisable, but also to have a clear 'national identity': a young, modern fashion brand could only be truly authentic if it held an element of its country's own culture. From that moment, Paul Smith was presented by the media — and by himself — as a 'True Brit'. His menswear and women's ranges blend traditional British tailoring with street-style details, and he combines them with a sense of humour, which earned him the title of the 'John Cleese of fashion'.[16] His humour is particularly prominent in his campaigns and invitations — such as the invitation from 1994 which featured an image of an electric fan to underline his 'coolness'. Notably, the photos accompanying a collection's invitations are nearly always supplied by Paul Smith himself, and they have often provided him with inspiration for the collection in question. He has incorporated a floral print from some old curtains, for example, into the lining for his garments and subsequently used the same pattern on the invitation. One stipulation Smith places on the photography is that the images may not be digitally manipulated. Craftsmanship is important to Paul Smith; different camera effects, printing techniques and graphics processing methods can be used, but the result must remain 'true to technique'. Hence the fourteen-colour pinstripe is never developed on the computer, but is instead created using actual threads every time. "Smith's style is deeply nostalgic and yet also progressive and avant-garde; he is steeped in British sartorial tradition and yet disrupts conventional design aesthetics and scrambles fashion's signs and symbols — the floral suit, the photo-printed budgie waistcoat, the strip-cartoon trousers, the pistachio-coloured tweeds."[17]

The same image also appears on his invitations, billboards and store

15 Alison Goodrum, *The National Fabric. Fashion, Britishness, Globalization*. Berg, Oxford 2005, p. 87.

16 Alison Goodrum, ibid. p. 86.

17 Alison Goodrum, ibid. p. 88.

18 Alison Goodrum, ibid. p. 122.

Paul Smith for Mini Cooper, 1997

designs. Panelling creates a classic ambience in all Paul Smith stores, while display cases featuring children's toys and packaging alongside paintings by modern artists result in an interesting mix of themes. In this way, even his stores fuse classic with avant-garde, whilst "at the same time another set of vocabularies is superimposed on the top of this aesthetic of traditionalism, namely notions of irony, kitsch and the surreal."[18]

CONCLUSION

The approach to building up a brand image varies considerably from one fashion name to another. However, the contributions from Marco Pecorari and Tamsin Blanchard in this book illustrate the irrefutable fact that all fashion brands, from avant-garde to classic couture houses, have been focusing on developing a clear image and visual identity since the Eighties.[19] In the late Nineties, fashion houses and luxury brands steeped in tradition decided to play their 'heritage card' in their rejuvenation process, enlisting the help of artists and designers and exploring all manner of innovative ways to update their monograms and logos. More avant-garde names such as Viktor & Rolf and Paul Smith have built their brand image around the philosophy that they want the brand to convey. In Paul Smith's case, he embodies a sense of British fashion history and culture, while Viktor & Rolf's conceptual, critical approach to the fashion industry runs through all aspects of their identity: their 'upside down' store in Milan was a perfect example of that, and could be seen as an extension of the surrealism theme which inspired the seal logo.

In this context, it is interesting to cover one more version of a brand image: the anti-brand, such as Maison Martin Margiela and A.F. Vandevorst have presented in recent decades. Maison Martin Margiela's response to logo mania is to stitch a blank label into all garments, although ironically the 4 stitches used to do so are visible on the outside and so distinct that the Maison Martin Margiela brand is immediately identifiable. The same holds for the way in which Maison Margiela prefers to use plain white for its packaging, its store design and its advertising, and drape everything in white cotton fabric, as if covering pieces of furniture in an empty house. This kind of anti-branding has since evolved into the brand's recognisable visual style. Meanwhile, the Belgian duo A.F. Vandevorst started their brand with a red cross as the logo stitched into their creations. They claimed to have been inspired by the world of hospitals and in particular by the work of Joseph Beuys. Over the years, they have shaped their universe more explicitly, including opening a pop-up store, *The Smallest Travelling Store In The World (TSTSITW)*, in the style of a hospital room which featured nothing more than a hospital bed, a monitor, a nightstand and a display case. Despite being built around an anti-ideology, we can conclude that these final two examples work as a 'total look' and are recognisable to a wider audience. Even here, the brand's form and message fit together seamlessly.

19 See the articles by Marco Pecorari and Tamsin Blanchard elsewhere in this book.

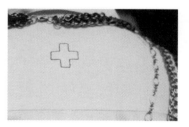

Above: Maison Martin Margiela logo
Below: A.F. Vandevorst logo, based on the Red Cross sign

The legendary *grande dame* of fashion Gabrielle 'Coco' Chanel (1883–1971), was renowned for her ground-breaking innovations which revolutionised women's fashion, jewellery, perfumes and handbags. Her emancipated approach to doing business and her outspoken opinions on fashion were equally significant in helping her to achieve legendary status. The two black, inter-locking letters 'C' and the Chanel brand name printed entirely in capitals speak for themselves.

Karl Lagerfeld, creative director since 1983, has managed to reorganise the Chanel fashion house without detracting from Chanel's numerous successes and recognisable signature pieces, such as the LBD (little black dress), the maritime and sporting influences, the use of unusual details like the gold-link chain and imitation jewellery, and her iconic bag designs such as the *2.55*. Lagerfeld introduced innovative interpretations of her tweeds in black, white and pink. He rescued Chanel from its own impending downfall and transformed it into one of the world's most luxurious and profitable fashion houses.

Over the course of almost three decades, Karl Lagerfeld has succeeded in creating a highly recognisable graphic style for the fashion house by consistently applying it in each and every Chanel-branded design.

A haughty Francophile, Karl Lagerfeld has continually displayed an unwavering sense of *zeitgeist* and incorporated it into the fashion house's approach through smart collaborations with hip and trendy musicians, artists and graphic designers who — just like Coco Chanel herself — personify the look of the moment.

Lagerfeld is constantly searching for ways to ensure Chanel's immortality by doing things that no other fashion house has done before. Examples include the most expensive TV advertisement ever made featuring Nicole Kidman in the lead role for *Chanel No. 5*, financing big-screen movies such as *Coco avant Chanel*, or staging fantastically theatrical fashion shows with extreme decors: from imported floes of ice and a magical underwater world to a maze of heavily laden buffet tables and an enormous wedding cake as the catwalk for his models. Lagerfeld attracted further attention in 2007 with the futuristic, travelling *Mobile Art Museum* which he commissioned from architecture virtuoso Zaha Hadid to mark the famous *2.55* leather handbag's 50th anniversary. Karl Lagerfeld is known as the *Kaiser* of the fashion world, and rightly so, because it seems the Chanel universe knows no bounds.   www.chanel.com

CHANEL

Clockwise from top to bottom:
Chanel advertisement, S/S 2012,
Chanel S/S 2011, Chanel S/S 2006,
Chanel advertisement, early Nineties

Clockwise from top to bottom:
Burberry advertisements, photographed by Mario Testino, 2005 and 2004
Burberry logo
Burberry advertisement, photographed by Mario Testino, S/S 2010
The famous Burberry check print

Having made its name with the iconic trench coat, the British label Burberry has since grown into a respected fashion house. Burberry's was founded in 1856 by Thomas Burberry and was initially focused on outerwear. In 1880, he introduced gabardine, a water-repellent yet breathable fabric. Thomas Burberry opened his first shop in 1891 on London's Haymarket, and Burberry's logo displaying an image of an equestrian knight and the Latin word Prorsum, meaning 'forwards', was developed in 1901. 1914 saw the creation of the first trench coat on behalf of the British government ; it formed part of the uniform for officers in the British Army. The renowned Burberry check, a pattern comprising beige, red, white and black, was designed in the 1920s and was used as lining for the trench coats.

The Seventies marked the start of a gradual decline of Burberry's chic image, and the brand came to be favoured predominantly by Britain's working-class youngsters, derisively termed 'chavs'. As a result, the fashion house launched a rebranding exercise in the late Nineties. The first step was to change the name from Burberry's to Burberry. Photographer Mario Testino, famous for his seductive fashion shots, was hired for the advertising campaigns and chose England's most famous supermodel Kate Moss for his very first campaign. Testino continues to shoot Burberry's advertising campaigns to this day, always using high-profile British models or actors.

Christopher Bailey was appointed as creative director in 2001 and promoted to chief creative officer in 2009, which gave him responsibility for all of the fashion house's creative activities, from the designs and their labels to packaging and the website. Since Bailey has been in charge at Burberry, the company has enjoyed tremendous growth, thanks in no small part to the arrival of Rose Marie Bravo as CEO in 2006. The key to the success of Bailey's designs lies in his ability to combine Burberry's sense of British heritage with contemporary style. While the trench coat has remained, it is given a new twist each season. The famous Burberry check is still a familiar sight too — not only on the inside of their trench coats, but also on packaging materials, clothes' labels and printed on Burberry bags.

In the fashion world, Burberry is a front runner in the use of social media. The label was the first to offer live streaming of its fashion show, for instance. And for the Spring/Summer 2012 collection, Burberry launched the 'Tweetwalk' which presented backstage photos of each of the new collection's looks on Twitter first, just before they headed down the catwalk.

www.burberry.com

Burberry store in Beijing, China

MAISON MARTIN MARGIELA *proper noun, plural*, derived from the name of a Belgian stylist. **Fashion company** created in **Paris** in 1988. Registered office situated at number 163 rue Saint Maur, 75011, Paris. Known for its taste for **transgression**, its fashion shows in unexpected places, its "street casting" mixing all ages. Categorised successively as underground, deconstructive, destroy, grunge, minimalist, provocative, established. ♦ **1°** Garments for women, offering several collections, from ready-to-wear fashion to unique pieces (*Artisanal* collection). The main collection uses a plain *white label** with no writing, sewn into the garments by hand with four *white stitches**. The other collections, of which there are 12, are identified by a circled number on the label. ♦ **2°** Male clients have also been taken care of since 1998, with four distinct collections. ♦ **3°** Communicates exclusively in the first person plural "we", in order to focus attention on *team-work** (16 nationalities) and to respect the creator's wish for *anonymity**. *"The only thing we wish to push to the forefront is our fashion".* ♦ **4°** Known for its taste for *recovery** and *recycling** of materials. ♦ **5°** May go as far as to re-release an existing garment (*Replicas**). ♦ **6°** Since its creation, has favoured the use of *whites**: walls, floors, stands, accessories, hanging wardrobes, in its boutiques, showrooms and offices. ♦ **7°** Its employees wear *white coats** (from "haute couture" workshops) as a "uniform" when serving the public. ♦ **8°** *Ext.* Sunglasses, jewellery, perfumes. ♦ **9°** A study subject in fashion schools. ♦ **10°** Name used internationally in books, articles and exhibitions.

Left: the definition of Maison Martin Margiela
Below: one of Maison Martin Margiela's infamous white labels
Right: Maison Martin Margiela collection definition

Belgian designer Martin Margiela (1957) set up his Maison Martin Margiela label together with Jenny Meirens in 1988, after graduating from the Royal Academy of Fine Arts in Antwerp. In 2002, the label was acquired by Diesel owner Renzo Rosso. In 2009 it was announced that Margiela had left the label several years previously, and that a young creative team was now behind the designs.

At the core of the Margiela design process is the desire to examine what clothing actually is, with the focus on its construction. This translates into over-blown proportions, clearly visible seams, lining and hems, garments being left intentionally unfinished, and existing items of clothing being deconstructed into something new. In Martin Margiela's time at the helm, he very rarely — if ever — gave interviews, and he stayed out of the public eye so as not to detract attention from the garments themselves. His tradition of presenting his designs on models wearing blindfolds could be seen as an extension of this approach. Nor do the labels in his garments make a direct reference to the fashion house. Instead, they are plain white labels simply displaying numbers: 0 stands for the artisanal women's collection, for example, and 22 indicates shoes. One external telltale sign of a Margiela design are four tiny white lines, the stitches holding the label in place on the garment's reverse.

www.maisonmartinmargiela.com

0 1 2 3 4 5 6 7 8 9
10 11 12 13 14 15 16
17 18 19 20 21 22 23
Maison Martin Margiela
PARIS

(0) Collection Artisanale for women & men

The défilé collection for women *

(1) The collection for women

(4) A wardrobe for women

(10) The collection for men

(14) A wardrobe for men

(11) A collection of accessories for women & men

(22) A collection of shoes for women & men

(8) Eyewear collection

(13) Objects & publications

MM⑥ Garments for ♀

* Totally white labe

A.F. VANDEVORST

FIRST WOMEN'S COLLECTION WINTER 98-99

SHOW
THURSDAY 12 MARCH 1998, 5PM
L'UNION FRATERNELLE DES METALLURGISTES
SALLE DE CONFERENCE
94, RUE JEAN-PIERRE TIMBAUD, 75011 PARIS
METRO: COURONNES

SHOWROOM: FROM 13 UNTIL 17 MARCH 1998
C/O D.V.N.
3 BIS, RUE DU PLÂTRE, 75004 PARIS
TEL: 01-42 74 75 70

PRESS AGENT: SYLVIE GRUMBACH
15, RUE D'ABOUKIR, 75002 PARIS
TEL: 01-42.33.93.18 & FAX: 01-40.26.43.53

A.F. VANDEVORST
WOLFSTRAAT 26, 2018 ANTWERP, BELGIUM
TEL: 32-3-272 19 56 & FAX: 32-3-272 26 13

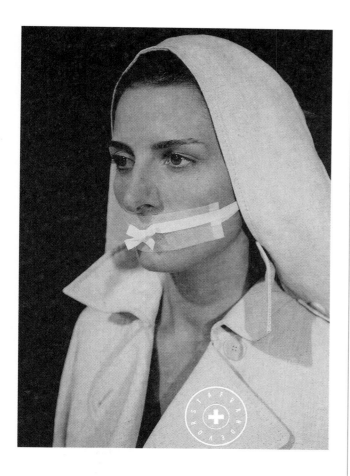

An Vandevorst and Filip Arickx met on their first day at the Fashion Department of the Academy of Fine Arts in Antwerp in 1987 and, discovering they shared a passion for collecting Red Cross paraphernalia, quickly became friends. Some ten years later, the duo launched their own label, A.F. Vandevorst, and presented their first collection in Paris.

A.F. Vandevorst's designs are sober with military influences, aimed at the 'urban nomad'. Their interest in the Red Cross remains to this day, and has found expression in their logo: the red outline of a cross. Their fascination for this organisation's imagery is rooted in their love for the work of, and the myth surrounding, the artist Joseph Beuys. The story goes that as a pilot in the Second World War, Beuys crash-landed in Russia and was rescued by members of a nomadic tribe who greased his body with animal fat and wrapped him in felt. These elements would later feature repeatedly in Beuys's work, along with a red cross which he used as his logo. Likewise, the Beuys themes can be clearly found in A.F. Vandevorst's designs. In addition, the duo's collections frequently contain references to Russia, another major source of inspiration, in the use of military influences, fur and black boots, for instance.

A.F. Vandevorst's most recent project is a pop-up shop concept designed as a miniature hospital entitled *TSTSITW*, which stands for *The Smallest Travelling Store in the World*.

www.afvandevorst.be

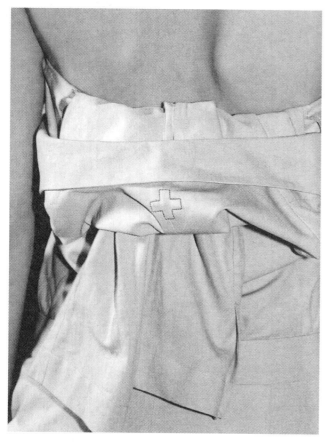

Above: A.F. Vandevorst, S/S 2007
Below: A.F. Vandevorst, A/W 2003–2004

While it was never his ambition to do so, Sir Paul Smith (1946), originally a racing cyclist, has become one of England's most successful designers. After growing up in Nottingham and leaving school at fifteen with no qualifications, he happened to get a job in a department store. There, he unearthed a hidden talent for window dressing, and his skill and ambition resulted in him being promoted to chief buyer for the menswear department at the age of just seventeen. But it was above all the group of 'arty' friends he hung out with in the local pub who introduced him to fashion design and the artistic movements that were emerging the 1960s: pop art, streetwear, pop music and industrial design. Evening classes at a local fashion college and various supplementary jobs in the fashion world helped him to hone his keen sense of marketing and tailoring. In 1970 he joined forces with his girlfriend Pauline Denyer to open his first store Paul Smith Vêtement Pour Homme, the only shop outside London to stock men's fashion by names such as Kenzo and Margaret Howell. He soon started selling his own designs too, which he made a point of employing local craftspeople and companies to produce. After the launch of his first menswear collection in Paris in 1976, his classic yet distinctive men's suits — with their unusual touches in terms of details, lining, use of colour or cut — subsequently became an international hit. Paul Smith presented his first women's line, featuring classic male tailoring, in London in 1994, and later added children's wear, denim wear, eyewear and a range of interior furnishings to his collections. Nowadays, Paul Smith comprises thirteen stand-alone brands for a variety of target groups, including exclusive tailored suits and high-end women's fashion.

But Paul Smith's activities are not limited to fashion alone: cameras, toys, umbrellas, cricket balls, books, curtains, pens, diaries, chairs, stamps, collectables and more, all featuring his unmistakable fourteen-colour pinstripe design, have extended his design repertoire, so that Paul Smith has become an overarching 'brand experience'. His shops and flagship stores in Asia, America and Europe all reflect Paul Smith's personality, evolution and lifestyle, yet each and every one of them is unique. To this day, he con-tinues to exert final control, both creatively and commercially, over his all-encompassing design portfolio.

www.paulsmith.co.uk

Above: Paul Smith's multi-colour logo by Alan Aboud
Below: Invitation for Paul Smith by Alan Aboud, A/W 2008–2009

Clockwise from top to bottom:
Paul Smith advertisement, S/S 2009,
Invitations for Paul Smith, both designed by
Alan Aboud, S/S 2002 and S/S 2005

Paul Smith

PAUL SMITH

PLAYERS
PAUL SMITH WOMEN SPRING SUMMER TWO THOUSAND AND TWO
ONLY

Paul Smith
WOMEN

PAUL SMITH WOMEN
SPRING / SUMMER 2005

VIKTOR & ROLF INVITE YOU TO ATTEND THE S/S 07 SHOW MON OCT AT 1.30 P

CARROUSEL DU LOUVRE, SALLE DELORME
99 RUE DE RIVOLI, 75001 PARIS
PRESS/ KARLA OTTO   T 0033142613436/ F 0033142615891
COMMERCIAL/ GIBO   T 0039025748061/ F 00390257480650

Left: invitation for Viktor & Rolf by Mevis & Van Deursen, S/S 2007
Right: Viktor & Rolf, S/S 2011

Viktor Horsting (1969) and Rolf Snoeren (1969) are conceptual masters of fashion. Each of their collections is built around a decisive vision and progressive idea, and every show demonstrates their sheer control of conceptual genius: clear, consistent and austere. The duo met while studying fashion at the ArtEZ Institute of the Arts in Arnhem, united by their shared passion for the visual arts and conceptualism. They both graduated in 1992. They spent a year gaining work experience at the Maison Martin Margiela fashion house, renowned for its deconstructive designs and controversial approach to fashion. The philosophy held great appeal for Horsting and Snoeren, as did the idea of setting up their own fashion house based on the French model.

Viktor & Rolf started out with autonomous fashion installations on the Paris art scene, which set the tone for their subsequent careers: the volumes, contrasts, layers, deconstruction and stark concepts in their fashion silhouettes all clamoured for attention. Wearability ranked second; feeding off their ambivalence towards the state of the fashion industry, the impact of their critical concept was more important.

The Viktor & Rolf luxury fashion label has been one of the most high-profile names in the international fashion world for more than ten years now, thanks to its alternative ideas, its 'total work' approach, the use of a recognisable, graphic visual language and the role of art direction in enabling the label to constantly evolve. The concept is truly all-encompassing; it is all about branding and luxury, and everything is styled — right down to Horsting's and Snoeren's appearance.

Details which make the Viktor & Rolf style so unmistakable include the recurrence of colours like pink, black and white, the use of ribbons and bows, and the wax seal logo, as well as the paradigms they create, such as upside down, light and dark, and real and virtual. Such themes run throughout their choice of fabrics, prints, decors, invitations and store design.

www.viktor-rolf.com

Top: Viktor & Rolf with Kristen McMenamy, A/W 2010–2011
Middle: Viktor & Rolf, menswear A/W 2010–2011
Bottom: Viktor & Rolf, menswear S/S 2011

Invitation for Raf Simons by Tom Tosseyn, A/W 2011–2012

'Rise of the craftsman, fall of the prince' was the slogan for Belgian fashion designer Raf Simons's Autumn/Winter 2011–2012 collection. While the words 'Rise of the craftsman' expressed his intention to go it alone as an independent fashion house, the phrase 'fall of the prince' appeared to be a critical observation of the current state of the fashion world, namely that the creative process and craftsmanship should never be overshadowed by fashion's commercial side. This was not the first time Simons had made such a statement; since the start of his seventeen-year career, the Belgian has been using visual (fashion) language to present his ideas and to communicate his beliefs. They relate not only to everyday fashion trends, but also to the world of fashion as a whole. For Raf Simons, fashion is all about using clothing to communicate, with music, photography and video as additional vehicles for expression. He regards fashion not as a monologue, but instead as the starting point for a conversation between creative individuals — between the maker and the wearer, and between the present and the past.

In Simons's view, fashion (i.e. communication) is primarily about emotions, behaviour and identity, which is why he incorporates a wide range of different media in his work. The conversation Simons wishes to enter into with his audience is manifested not only in his clothing, but also in how his shows, stores and exhibitions are designed, in his video presentations, in the style of his promotional materials, publications and invitations, the prints on his garments, his website and even his choice of music. Film, in particular, has played a key role right from the start of his career. He presented his first collections inside galleries using videos: they featured documentary-style footage of young people on the street dressed in his clothing designs. Even now, Simons continues to use video for promotional purposes and to document his design process. He records the model-casting sessions, the clothes fittings and the hair and make-up sessions for his shows, and subsequently shares the films on his website. Instead of merely providing an insight into the amount of work involved in putting on a show, it seems as if he is challenging his audience to view fashion as a series of performances rather than just a stand-alone end product. Raf Simons also draws heavily on music to provide inspiration for his collections and to intensify the audience experience during the show. Band names and song lyrics feature in all manner of ways, such as in the titles of his collections, in the prints on his clothes and in the invitation layouts. His shows are visual extravaganzas featuring several models wearing identical outfits, marching in line like soldiers, not uncommonly carrying flags, ban-

ners, torches or blankets, perhaps adorned with tattoos or with their faces partially obscured. His fashion designs are sometimes presented in everyday places — on the streets, in a park or in a school playground — while on other occasions he selects special locations such as the Cité des sciences et de l'industrie science museum in Paris. Hence, every show is an almost tangible experience that works with the collection to form a visual entity, with his audience being absorbed into his total multimedia work of fashion. In order to achieve this, he often enlists the help of graphic designers, photographers, film-makers, product designers and musicians. His preferred way of developing his visual idiom is to collaborate with friends, heroes and colleagues, working with them to redefine and reinterpret the same fundamental ideas.

Ultimately, his fashion centres around three recurring themes. Firstly, his fascination for youth, which can be seen in his use of street models. Secondly, there is a repeated yearning for independence; this manifests itself not only in his interest in teenage rebellion, but also in his own attitude towards the fashion business. Thirdly his focus on his craft, an example of which is the patchwork effect on many of his garments. His posters, invitations, quilts and the accoutrements carried by the models also underline his unbounded, experimental approach to design. His development can be described in terms of several distinct periods.

THE FIRST PERIOD: A FASCINATION FOR REBELLIOUS TEENAGERS

Raf Simons began his career in 1995 with teenager Robbie Snelders as his first, and great, muse. Together with Robbie, their friend and artist Peter de Potter, and photographer Willy Vanderperre, Simons created photos, text and collages. In this period, Raf Simons focused on the relationship between recalcitrant teenagers, their parents and society as a whole. In his videos, clothing and prints, he tried to capture their views of the world and help others to understand them. They were involved in the alternative subcultures of the Eighties and early Nineties, such as punk, new wave, Britpop, house, acid and rave. As a result, references to these subcultures and the music, films and styles associated with them formed the basis for Raf Simons's visual language in his early period, as illustrated by the titles of his collections: 'Three boys and a girl hanging out at home, talking, fooling around, playing records', 'We only Come out at Night', 'How to Talk to your Teen', 'Black Palms', 'Radioactivity', 'Kinetic Youth', 'Disorder Incubation Isolation', and 'Summa Cum Laude'.

Left: Raf Simons advertisement,
photographed by Pierre Debusschere,
A/W 2012–2013
Top: Raf Simons, *Woe Onto Those
Who Spit On The Fear Generation…
The Wind Will Blow It Back*, S/S 2002
Middle: Raf Simons, *Rise Of The Craftsman
Fall Of The Prince*, A/W 2011–2012
Bottom: Raf Simons, film still from *Safe*,
by Willy Vanderperre

His focus on teenagers attracted attention, and Raf Simons soon experienced a breakthrough, particularly outside the fashion industry. At the exhibition curated by Terry Jones — '2001 (minus 3)' —, Simons presented a living module centred around three teenagers acting just as they would at home. In 1999, he created several outfits for the Belgian alternative rock band dEUS, and in 2001 he accepted the opportunity to present his view of the teenage world as guest editor of *i-D* magazine. Raf Simons rounded off his adolescent-oriented period with an ode to valiant teenagers in his series of photographs called 'Isolated Heroes'. By focusing on the face rather than the clothes, the effect was of him wanting to record and immortalise the character of every boy who had inspired him. Notably, all the boys shared a similar look: distinctive and sharply defined bone structure, edgy semi-shaved geometric hairstyles, and indiscernible gazes, dreamy, yet with a hint of aggression — male images which went on to typify the Raf Simons universe.

THE SECOND PERIOD: THE CRITICAL ADOLESCENT — RAF SIMONS'S ARMY STRIKES BACK

After a sabbatical, Raf Simons returned to fashion in 2001, this time with a focus on more mature adolescents. Seeing them as driven by idealism and a determination to change the world, Raf Simons sent out a political message by portraying them as an army of progressive warriors who were prepared to fight for their shared ideals. With his bomber jackets and camouflage prints, and with hoods and scarves obscuring faces, Raf Simons introduced a contemporary uniform for young idealists. In his recognisable graphic style, inspired by anti- and non-conformist beliefs, Raf Simons designed uniforms that functioned as vehicles for ideological statements against racism, authority and commercialism.

The adolescents in question were different from the teenagers in Raf Simons's first period: they were earnest, unwavering in their conviction, politically aware and prepared to act. This adolescent period differed from his previous period in terms of visual language and performance too. The style became tighter and more direct, and text assumed a more prominent role. His shows featured more drama, created by the use of scaffolding, smoke machines and flaming torches. Raf Simons presented his 'army' in collections including 'Riot, Riot, Riot', 'Woe onto those who spit on the fear generation... the wind will blow back', 'Consumed' and 'Closer'.

Mirroring the teenagers as they matured, Raf Simons himself evolved from a rebel into an influential and respected fashion designer. The teenagers became young professionals, and the Raf Simons fashion house metamorphosed into a company with a business model. 2008 marked the start of collaborations with established names such as Fred Perry, Eastpak, Dr. Martens and Linda Farrow, and a ready-to-wear line, 'RAF by Raf Simons', was launched around the same time. Characteristic of this period were the young men in streamlined suits demonstrating a trendy twist to the classic cut. They offered young professionals a modern alternative. The collections mixed elements from the worlds of business and sport, combining classic and contemporary aesthetics, underlined by the use of more — and in particular bold — colours, minimalistic and geometric designs and the blend of high-tech materials with traditional fabrics. As a result of one image containing so many fragments and distractions, his visual idiom took on a futuristic feel. Pierre Debusschere's film of the design process, shot at one-second intervals, contributed to the multilayered structure. Meanwhile, the use of brilliant, almost acid, colours and new, self-designed fonts, introduced by graphic designer Tom Tosseyn and applied in prints on both clothing and paper, further emphasised the sense of futurism. Even the invitations received similar treatment, produced in an edgy mix of materials and techniques, resulting in novel combinations of stickers and paper, print, paint and spray cans, metal and cardboard, classic and self-designed fonts, and digital and artisan styles.

TIME FOR REFLECTION AND REVERTING TO THE PAST

In 2010, Raf Simons celebrated his fifteen-year anniversary with the Spring/Summer 2011 collection called 'How we would celebrate our fifteenth anniversary with you'. Blatantly referring to his own career, the name led to the end of the partnership with his business partner and financier. The Raf Simons fashion house opted to go it alone, and launched a new, second line entitled '1995'. This collection, which was based on Raf Simons's complete works, illustrated his creative development over the previous 17 years. With his Autumn/Winter 2011–2012 collection, he announced the rise of the craftsman and demonstrated his focus on independence and creativity. He communicated that message through his prints, through his use of the archetypical item of work clothing — the apron — and with symbolism such as hammers and crosses. The importance of craftsmanship could also be read into the printing method itself, which made it appear as if the images had been stamped. Even the finer points of the invitation — each of the four 1.5mm-thick side edges in a different colour — underlined his regard for the artisanal approach. Notably, Raf Simons takes a very broad view of his own craft, namely that of fashion: in addition to clothing, his collection includes home furnishings such as blankets, cushions and rugs.

The idea that fashion design is a gradual and evolutionary creative process featuring constant dialogue between the present and the past is at the very heart of Raf Simons's vision of fashion. In view of the development of the couture house so far, one can expect that Raf Simons will continue to fight for creativity and ideals in the fashion world, based on the conflicts between modern subcultures and society at large and between the new idealists and their predecessors.

www.rafsimons.com

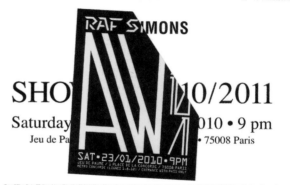

Above: invitation for Raf Simons by Tom Tosseyn, A/W 2010–2011
Below: invitation for Raf Simons by Tom Tosseyn, S/S 2012

Founded in 1854 by *malletier* Louis Vuitton (1821–1892), this luxurious, family-owned French fashion house is one of the grandest and most famous couture houses in the world. When it started out, the Louis Vuitton firm specialised in producing handmade suitcases, bags and accessories of the highest quality, characterised by their patented, status-boosting canvases: the golden brown checked Damier pattern dating from 1888 and the monogram pattern featuring the initials LV and three Venetian *quatrefoils* from 1896. The three flowers, the initials and the Damier canvas form the basis of the fashion house's visual brand identity, which not only appears regularly in its bags or in its garments, but also serves as inspiration for the company's global in-store design concept.

The Louis Vuitton organisation has always taken an inventive approach to using its house style and star status. It is not afraid to play around with its products, and has successfully reinvented itself several times in the past 150 years, without losing status or clientele.

Since the arrival of Marc Jacobs as creative director in 1997, the fashion house has repeatedly invited hip and trendy visual artists and celebrities to join Jacobs in producing new interpretations based on Louis Vuitton's intellectual property, thus supporting the firm in its quest for new target groups as well as providing its fans with new and limited 'must-haves'. From fashion design, jewellery, accessories, prints, colours, window-dressing materials and editorials, to complete works of art, everything the firm produces is kept in line with whatever the art direction for that season may be.

The most recent graphic design developments have been architectural ones. State-of-the-art buildings designed by leading architects and interior architects mean that even urban spaces are being used as a form of brand extension. This has turned architecture into a new frontier for luxurious fashion houses like Louis Vuitton, supporting their all-encompassing brand experiences and positions of power. In the world of the mighty Louis Vuitton it would appear that anything is possible.

www.louisvuitton.com

Clockwise from top to bottom:
Louis Vuitton flagship store in New York, decorated by Takashi Murakami, 2008; Louis Vuitton trunk; Louis Vuitton advertisement, photographed by Steven Meisel, S/S 2012; the famous Louis Vuitton monogram in the typical colour scheme

LOUIS VUITTON

47

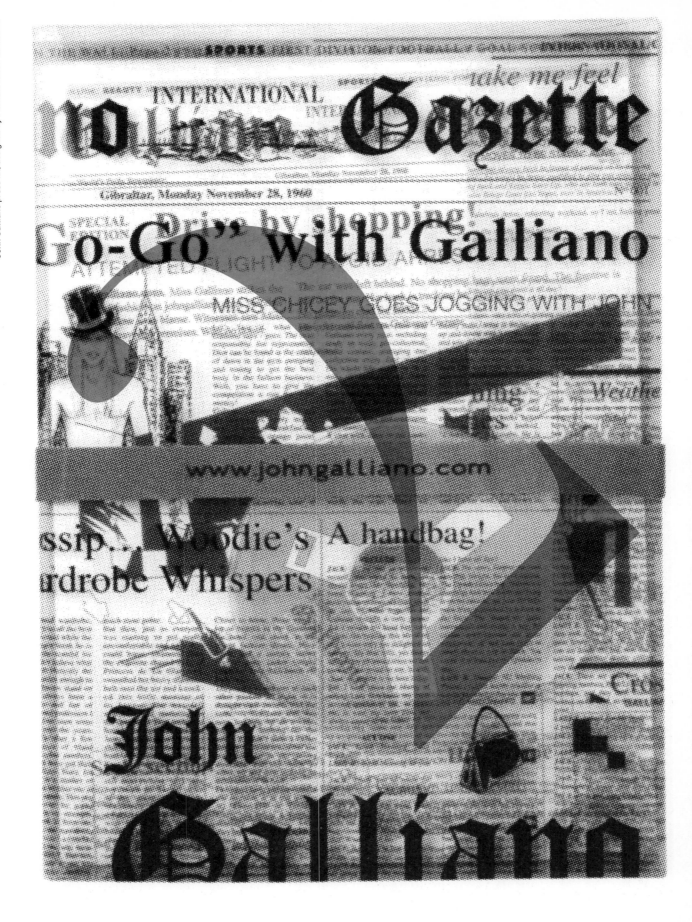

FASHION & GRAPHIC DESIGN

— TAMSIN BLANCHARD

It is just a tiny rectangle of fabric, sewn into the back of a jacket. But what power it holds. Tied up in that little label is money, aspiration, sex appeal and status. Unpick it, and the jacket might as well be worthless. The label has become its own form of currency. It is the maker's mark; the reason the garment was sold in the first place. In the fashion industry, it is all about labels, branding and identity. A simple label can mean the difference between a plain, white T-shirt selling for £5.99 or £59.99.

Increasingly, fashion brands rely on packaging and presentation rather than the product itself. The brand image defines a particular aspiration or set of references that attract the consumer to choose one polo shirt, one pair of jeans or a particular pair of trainers over another. There comes a point when designer clothing is not about cut and cloth, but about graphic design, pack-aging and communication, whether it is a rubber band sewn into the collar and stamped with John Galliano in Gothic script, or a catalogue for Yohji Yamamoto, photographed by Inez van Lamsweerde & Vinoodh Matadin and art directed by M/M (Paris), a collector's item in its own right, but seen only by a chosen few within the fashion industry. Not surprisingly, the graphic designer responsible for the look of a label or the art direction of the ad campaign has taken on a status and power within the fashion industry that was unheard of in the early Eighties.

Fashion companies have become mini publishing empires, often employing their own graphic design teams, and producing not just invitations to fashion shows, but 'lookbooks', catalogues, press mail-outs, magazines, advertisements and even Christmas cards. But this is all a relatively new phenomenon. And much of the material, although highly sophisticated, expensive to produce, exquisitely designed and highly influential, is totally ephemeral, and thrown away without another thought.

British maverick Peter Saville was one of the pioneers who paved the way for the current generation of fashion graphics. 'Be careful what you wish for' is his motto; he intends to blow it up large in neon, and hang it on his Clerkenwell studio wall. As a young graduate in post-punk, bombed-out Manchester,

Balenciaga advertisement by Inez van Lamsweerde & Vinoodh Matadin and M/M (Paris), S/S 2001

he wished for a time when the world would be a better place because of the way it was designed. It would look better, it would work better. Twenty-five years later, the landscape of not just Manchester, but of the whole consumer universe has changed beyond recognition. It has been designed. In Saville's opinion, it has gone too far. It has been over-designed, given a lick of gloss just for the sake of it. Things don't necessarily look better. They certainly don't necessarily work any better. But one thing is for sure: they have been designed.

In the mid-Eighties, when Saville began collaborating with photographer Nick Knight and creative director Marc Ascoli on the advertising and imagery for Yohji Yamamoto, the concept of a graphic designer working on a fashion brand, creating layouts of images for brochures to be sent to press and buyers, deciding on the size and position of a logo, or simply editing a set of pictures, was something quite new. When Nick Knight requested that Saville work on the Yamamoto project with him, the idea was met with some degree of puzzlement. Nobody was quite sure what exactly a graphic designer would do. But the collaboration between Knight and Saville was to prove groundbreaking. "When the Yohji catalogues appeared on the scene in Autumn/Winter 1986, they had a really profound effect," remembers Saville. "They became collected immediately because they were different. When you look back at them now, they are actually a little bit naive by contemporary graphic standards."

The fashion industry is one of the most overcrowded and competitive industries. What makes one designer's white shirt stand out from another's is not necessarily the design. An architect might be attracted to a shirt by Comme des Garçons because of the message it is communicating to him or her. The way that message is communicated is carefully coded in language he will understand, through the advertising, the label, the packaging, the store design – it's a matter of presentation rather than fashion. Likewise, a businessman might buy his shirt from Hugo Boss because the logo speaks to him. It is confident, direct and has a very clear, corporate message. However similar the shirts may be, their customers live in totally different worlds.

Graphics have become an integral part of any fashion house; in some cases, the graphic designer or art director is also the fashion designer. Giorgio Armani for instance, is the all-seeing eye for his label: both art director and fashion director. "A designer label is his or her business card," he says. "It not only reflects the spirit and integrity of each collection; it also expresses the philosophy and character of the line to the customer. The final product is the most important part of the package, but a label and logo secures a recognisable identity. The graphic identity is a natural extension to what my products are trying to express and reflect."

In many cases, the graphic designer takes on a role as important, if not more important, than the fashion designers themselves. As creative director of Burberry, Fabien Baron was closely involved in many aspects of the British brand's relaunch at the end of the Nineties. Working alongside managing director Rose Marie Bravo, he signalled the new direction of the brand by not only modernising the logo (losing the confusing apostrophe in the process), but by creating an advertising campaign before there was any new product to advertise. His first ads for the brand, working with the photographer Mario Testino and promoting a certain English eccentricity and humour, were to set the tone for the rest of the highly successful turnaround of Burberry from a purveyor of old-fashioned raincoats to a dynamic, high-fashion, luxury label.

The Belgian designer Walter Van Beirendonck has always incorporated graphics into his fashion, both for his own labels and for the streetwear brand, W&LT, with the help of Paul Boudens, the Antwerp-based graphic designer who has worked with many of the new wave of Belgian designers since the late Eighties. Van Beirendonck sees graphics and fashion as so inseparable as to include graphics as part of the fashion degree for students at the prestigious Antwerp Academy of Fine Arts. "It is an important 'first presentation' to the real world," he says. "A graphic communication identity is important because it is the impression and language between designer and public."

When Stella McCartney launched her own label under the Gucci umbrella in 2002, she worked with Wink Media, the multidisciplinary creative agency set up in London by Tyler Brulé in 1998 to define her identity in terms of a graphic logo. Her debut show was held in March 2002, at the École des Beaux Arts in Paris. It was as though she was starting with a blank canvas; the catwalk was bright white and her new logo, her name apparently punched out as a series of dots, was emblazoned across it in silver. Although the assembled press and buyers were very familiar with Stella McCartney's name, this was the first time they would see a fully fledged collection bearing it.

Erik Torstensson is one of a team of art directors at Wink Media. Wink offers a wide range of creative services, including advertising, brand development and corporate identity. But Stella McCartney was a unique project. "We were creating a new brand for a very well-known designer, so it was already loaded with values and perceptions, which made it very interesting, but also much more demanding, as the expectations on Stella launching her own label were very high." His job was to create a brand image for a designer who already had a very strong brand image of her own. Everybody knew who Stella McCartney was, but nobody knew what her fashion label looked like. The process was a collaboration between Torstensson, McCartney and typeface designer Richard Hart. "We worked very closely with Stella to explore different directions based on her personal style and professional requirements," says Torstensson. "We would often visit Stella's studio to study the fabrics and the designs so we could get a very clear idea of the collection – and of course the designer behind it." The initial brief was to create a logotype for the launch of a brand with her own name. "The logo had not only to convey a sense of luxury but also the freshness, quality, charm and edge that are embodied in the spirit of Stella McCartney's designs. It was also important that the logo would have longevity, versatility and accessibility to different markets." McCartney might be based in London, but Gucci is an international luxury-goods group and the new label had to have the same appeal in Dubai as in New York, Sydney or Tokyo.

W&LT – Wild & Lethal Trash! by Walter Van Beirendonck, S/S 1993

A brand's graphic identity is how it expresses itself, shows what it wants to belong to and talks to its customer with its chosen visual language. The graphic identity will be applied to everything that the brand uses, so it is vital

Top: Stella McCartney advertisement photographed by Mert & Marcus, S/S 2012
Middle: Stella McCartney advertisement photographed by Ryan McGinley, A/W 2009–2010
Below right: Yves Saint Laurent advertisement
photographed by Inez van Lamsweerde &
Vinoodh Matadin, A/W 2009–2010

to find an expression that suits its values. If your brand has a well-produced and managed graphic identity or design strategy, it will pay off tenfold. A badly managed and implemented corporate identity can prove to be very expensive and damaging. The responsibility, therefore, is on the designer to get it right. An identity for a brand like Stella McCartney must be as confident and sure of itself as the woman behind it.

For any fashion house, a well-designed, universally recognised logo is the key to commercial success. The logo becomes its own currency, whether printed on a T-shirt, embossed on a wallet, packaged around a face cream or, of course, sewn into an item of clothing. No one has proved this better than Yves Saint Laurent, who has one of the most famous and enduring logos in fashion history. He was one of the first to turn to a graphic artist for help in translating the abstract idea of a new fashion house into a logo. Yves Saint Laurent had met A.M. Cassandre through his previous employer, Christian Dior, and he approached the old master (who was already well known for his stylish, graphic posters for Dubonnet and the *Normandie* ocean liner) in the late Fifties to create his own logo. It is said to have taken just a few minutes for Cassandre to sketch the three letters Y, S and L into their elegant, interlocking shape. Those three letters, beautifully and timelessly drawn, were to form the basis of one of the most prestigious and lucrative fashion houses ever. Even people who have never owned a Saint Laurent handkerchief, let alone a piece of haute couture, could draw the logo from memory.

Alice Rawsthorn, director of the Design Museum in London and author of *Yves Saint Laurent – A Biography*, says the YSL logo is successful because it is a beautiful piece of lettering. "It is exquisitely drawn in an instantly recognisable but distinctive style. Also, its central characteristics — elegance and a sleek sensuality — fuse perfectly with those of the brand and it has been reproduced more or less consistently over the years. Those are the generic characteristics of any classic logo and the YSL symbol encapsulates them perfectly." The logo is so strong, that when the Gucci Group took control of the brand in 2000, it was one of the few things that was not revamped. "Even a visual obsessive like Tom Ford has restrained himself to making just a few tiny tweaks since the Gucci Group took control of YSL," says Rawsthorn. "Everything else about the company has changed — but not the logo." Fabien Baron is not surprised that Tom Ford didn't change the logo: "I would not have changed it either. Cassandre was one of the best graphic designers in the world. He was an artist. That logo can stay forever. It's beautiful. It's the lettering, the intricacy of the logo, the way the letters are stacked up. It's very elegant and very French with a sense of history. Why change it if it works? It would be like going to Egypt and changing the pyramids." (However, Hedi Slimane — who was appointed head of design in 2012 — decided to change the iconic logo in the autumn of 2012 – Ed. note)

It was in the Eighties, however, that fashion houses began to take graphic design and art direction seriously. Yohji Yamamoto's creative director, Marc Ascoli, was persuaded into hiring Peter Saville by Nick Knight, a photographer who had come to his attention after a series of one hundred portraits of the Eighties for *i-D* magazine. Saville's work with Manchester band Joy Division impressed Ascoli. "Marc had the confidence in the mid-Eighties to break new ground and break new photographers," says Saville. "Nick had never shot fashion before, his portraits for *i-D* were as close as he'd come to the style magazine world. But Marc would take a sports photographer if he wanted to because he knows he could put the clothes in front of the photographer and say just take the picture. That's how he started with Nick – he did a men's shoot. As I understand it, during the shoot, Nick asked who would be doing the graphics. Apparently Mark said, 'I don't know. What is the graphics?' He didn't really know what Nick meant. There was not a close relationship of any sort between graphic designer and fashion."

Joy Division, *Unknown Pleasures* album, 1979, cover designed by Peter Saville

The graphic designer was, however, already well-established in the music business. Stephanie Nash and Anthony Michael, who formed the design agency Michael Nash after they graduated from St Martins in the early Eighties, had made a name for themselves in the music industry long before they began their work with designers such as John Galliano, Alexander McQueen and Marc Jacobs. "I think we started off doing music – including work for Neneh Cherry and Massive Attack — because in the early Eighties, there wasn't any fashion to be done," says Nash. "If somebody makes music and they have made a record, then you have a respect for that music. You have got to be their graphic designer in the same way that if you've made a frock, you've got to graphically represent that brand and that frock. You have got to do the same for the musician. I suppose we were doing it in a fashion, corporate identity kind of way and I think music sits in the middle and you do all these photo sessions and get heavily involved with the hairstyling and makeup." Despite the fact that they were at St Martin's School of Art around the same time as John Galliano, and remember him playing with Letraset for his logo in the college library, fashion and graphics students were not encouraged to work together. Nowadays it seems impossible to have one without the other. "It would have been a great experience doing the final show material for one of the students' shows." It was not until almost twenty years later that their paths crossed once more and Michael Nash Associates was commissioned to work on a new brand identity and packaging for Galliano, to coincide with the opening of the designer's first store.

Michaël Amzalag and Mathias Augustyniak, the French designers who formed the creative partnership M/M (Paris) in 1991, also work with both music and fashion. It is possible to trace the evolution between their 2001 cover for Björk's *Hidden Place* single and their two short but impactful seasons' worth of advertising images for Calvin Klein. The two clients could not be further apart – one is fairly specialist, artistic and independent and the other mass-market and corporate – but their markets are surprisingly similar. Fashion houses, no matter how mainstream, need to keep a step ahead if they are to maintain their credibility. M/M (Paris), with their playful, hands-on techniques, including drawing over images and scratching into photographs, have been incredibly influential in the late Nineties and into the new millennium. Their approach is the antithesis to that of Baron & Baron, who has had a long-standing, close working relationship with Calvin Klein. Baron's work for the company has always been clean, slick and utterly consistent. But M/M (Paris) had a completely different approach.

Björk, *Hidden Place* single, 2001, cover designed by M/M (Paris)

Calvin Klein advertisement by Inez van Lamsweerde & Vinoodh Matadin and M/M (Paris), S/S 2002

"The whole set-up needed a shake-up," says Amzalag. They like to work in bold statements rather than subtle nuances. Their way of making people sit up and take notice of the brand again — of injecting it with some credibility and freshness — was to take the Calvin Klein logo, the very core of the fashion empire, and rip it up and start again. They re-drew it, as a schoolkid might make a doodle in his exercise book. They felt the Calvin Klein brand had become schizophrenic and needed to have a single stamp to bring all the strands back together again. "The character of Calvin Klein had become like a ghost," they say. They wanted the logo to look as though someone had redrawn it from memory. The ads were no longer about the clothes. They were about rebranding a brand that had become so familiar it was almost invisible.

Previously, M/M (Paris) had worked for Yohji Yamamoto. In 1994 they were asked to design ads for the Y's diffusion range for which Peter Saville had drawn the logo. They were, of course, aware of Saville's previous work for the label, and their own work became an evolution of that. "Peter Saville was one of the first modern art directors," they say. "He understood that graphic design is about ideas. He is fed by different fields of creativity."

At their best, graphic designers have brought to the fashion industry another set of eyes, a fresh perspective and an uncompromising vision. At worst, they are simply another marketing tool, a way for the designer to create a visual peg on which to hang the sales of perfumes, face creams, scarves and T-shirts. In the early Nineties, when Saville's contract with Yohji Yamamoto came to an end, he thought there was nowhere else to go in the fashion industry, that it had become a dead end. "As we got to the end of the Eighties it all seemed really stupid and unnecessary, and there was a recession and it was nonsense really," says Saville. "At the time, I said, fashion clients are never going to pay a grand a day. I wrote the fashion business off as a new business area for graphic design. I just couldn't see it happening." But of course, the domino effect had only just begun. A whole new generation of graphic designers — and fashion designers — had been studiously collecting those Yohji Yamamoto catalogues, as well as Six, the groundbreaking magazine published by Comme des Garçons which was one of the defining moments of the fusion between fashion and graphics. "By the time we got to the mid-Nineties, I looked back and reconvened with fashion to see that, oh!, they've embraced the graphic element big time," says Saville. Fashion designers themselves, even the ones who were just starting out and still couldn't afford to pay a graphic designer, were having a go. "I looked at the scene in the mid-Nineties and fashion had really embraced graphics," he says. But perhaps it has gone too far. The design has overtaken the content. Although he says it is what he wished for, Saville confesses that he didn't really want it to turn out like this. "Design is the new advertising. It's the insidious influence. It was better when it was a form of rebellion, when you had to fight with business. Now it's the other way round. It's entirely superficial. The result of it all is that design loses its credibility, its truth. Rather than design communicating a certain integrity, it begins to be the opposite. If it looks good, don't trust it."

The whole process has certainly speeded up, and graphic designers are treated much the same as photographers are: with a certain awe and reverence, but also often with the same short shelf-life of a few seasons only. As the fashion

The groundbreaking magazine by Comme des Garçons, *Six* (Number 2), 1988

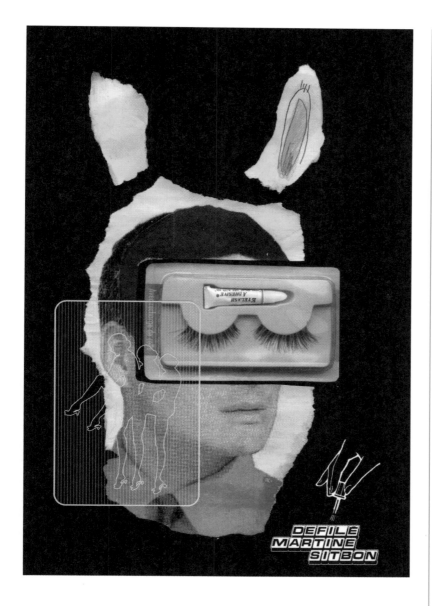

Invitations for Martine Sitbon by M/M
(Paris), various seasons

industry grows and grows, each company fighting for its slice of the action,
what they are saying become less important than how they are saying it. There
is a conflict of power between fashion and graphic designers. "What is more
powerful," asks Mathias Augustyniak of M/M (Paris), "the image or the object?"
Presentation is in danger of becoming everything.

Nevertheless, what is remarkable is that fashion graphics have become a
genre of their own, often existing in their own private universe occupied by the
fashion industry and rarely seeing the light of day beyond that. "Many times,
there are images that could have several lives," agrees Michael Amzalag. "In
fashion, once you've seen it, it's dead, which I think is stupid because it's not
dead. If you are a fashion addict, the idea is to have several cupboards and then
you store your old clothing, and then do some kind of rotation – you wait ten
years or five years, and pull it out again. It's just a matter of shifting things. Of
course you don't wear it with the same shoes."

'ZONES-IN-BETWEEN': THE ONTOLOGY OF A FASHION PRAXIS

— MARCO PECORARI

The catalogue of Yohji Yamamoto's A/W 1986–1987 collection portrayed the Italian painter Luciano Castelli wearing Yamamoto's creations while painting his own works. Angelo Figus's A/W 2002–2003 invitation took the shape of a vinyl record, whereas Maison Martin Margiela's invitations took the shape of a dish or a calendar. Prada's press releases for S/S 1992 were written by the visionary fashion writer Anna Piaggi, while Bernhard Willhelm's S/S 2003 press release appears in the form of a poem. All these examples are just a handful of the infinite variations that are continually materialising in fashion communication materials. A constant use of citations, the use of extravagant materials, and the collaborations with artists, writers and graphic designers are more than occasional events — they have become a consolidated practice in fashion communication. But what do these objects represent? Are they merely fashion communication devices which use some artistic practices to raise the profiles of designers' agencies? Indeed, a fruitful interpretation of the ontology of these materials might address these practices to the aim of constructing an image for a fashion designer's agency. This praxis usually involves a dissolution of the commercial attitude of these communicational materials, focusing on their symbolic character in order to direct the social perception of the fashion designer as an artist.

Invitation for Angelo Figus, A/W 2002–2003

Looking at the past, a clear example of this strategy can be seen in Paul Poiret's American commercial campaigns during the early teens of the last century. As the fashion historian Nancy Troy has shown in her *Couture Culture* (2004), Poiret's denial of any commercial intent and his disdain for publicity was part of his self-construction as an artist. Like an illusionist, the French couturier made the commercial and 'vulgar' mannequins disappear, substituting them for his wife, who wore his collections to all the important events that the couple attended. It is no coincidence that these happenings were also attended by potential buyers or influential members of the press. A camouflage of commercial devices and practices has, indeed, represented an important element in the construction of fashion designers' agencies as artists. However, it is also important to note that these practices have drastically changed their meaning towards the end of the last century, especially due to the rise of fashion design as a recognised discipline of our contemporary times. The landmarks of this change are often manifest in specific events: the *ArtForum* cover portraying Issey Miyake (February 1982), or the first exhibition dedicated to a living designer, Yves Saint Laurent, at the Metropolitan Museum in New York (1983).

The status of fashion and fashion designers has been drastically transformed in the last thirty years and this has inevitably influenced the construction of designers' agencies. This shift has brought about a wider analysis of the very practice of fashion, especially in relation to art. A seminal event was the Fashion Biennale *Art/Fashion* (1996), held in Florence and curated by Germano Celant and Luigi Settembrini. This was one of the first occasions to explore the relationships between art and fashion without the sort of overwrought symmetry typical of most art/fashion reflections during the Eighties and Nineties. Indeed, a common aporia of this new discourse on fashion was to compare fashion to art and thus put both disciplines into a vicious circle of parallelisms. To some extent, this tendency has paralysed the understanding of the dialogues between these two distinct disciplines, in some cases transforming the analysis into a void comparison of practices where fashion is represented as a sort of emulation or mimesis of art. Nevertheless, a few works have tried to subvert this attitude, presenting the peculiarity of fashion as a self-referential process of creation, approaching its relation to art through a reciprocal exchange — a dialogue, not a monologue.

An extreme example of this interpretation was *Dysfashional* (2007), a touring exhibition held for the first time in Luxembourg and curated by Luca Marchetti and Emanuele Quinz. This event aimed to reflect the thinking processes of designers, asking them to confront and translate their ideas through a diverse language. No clothes were exhibited. Whereas Maison Martin Margiela challenged the very concept of the fashion houses through the re-representation in loci of its maison in rue Saint-Maur (Paris), the Belgian designer Raf Simons created a video installation, *Repeat, 1995–2005*, a flashback on the duality of the main concepts developed in his career: black and white, adolescence and adulthood. The aim of *Dysfashional* was to show the 'dys-' suffix of fashion which characterises, according to its curators, a branch of contemporary fashion that is constantly involved in dialogues with diverse disciplines and their diverse languages. Fashion design is not perceived as art but as a process of creation that is not only embodied in dress, but can also assume diverse shapes that reflect a method of thinking. Hence, the results of such thinking can assume the shape of a dress, but also of an installation, a video, a fashion show, etcetera. In contemporary fashion the colossal creation of fashion materials, which are produced in parallel to the collection itself, seems to acquire more and more importance, especially due to the numerous collaborations that the creation of these objects involve. Although the dress still plays the role of protagonist, fashion designers are producing complete universes that require diverse languages to translate and fully represent their visions. Invitations, catalogues, press releases, fashion films, exhibitions and websites stimulate interaction with other disciplines, consequentially blurring the boundaries. Nowadays, collaborations with artists, graphic designers or writers are no

P/E 2006

6

P/E 2006

VENDREDI 7 OCTOBRE 2005
18H30

Stade Français
2, rue du Commandant Guilbaud
75016 PARIS

Porte de St Cloud

Maison Martin Margiela

Invitation for Maison Martin Margiela, S/S 2006

Image from a Yohji Yamamoto catalogue, photographed by Nick Knight, art direction by Marc Ascoli, A/W 1986–1987

longer perceived as attempts to elevate the social recognition of fashion designers, but rather as joint collaborations which actually modify fashion practices. Lately, fashion media materials have been significantly featured in many fashion exhibitions where entire sections are dedicated to invitations or catalogues, like in the exhibition *Future Beauty: 30 Years of Japanese Fashion*, held at the Barbican in London (2010). Despite this recent attention, only a handful of fashion museums actively collect and conserve these materials. Although ephemera are collected in diverse private or public museums or archives, fashion museums have mostly amassed them thanks to donations, and have used them as internal documentary sources to support the study of dress rather than as historical materials worthy of being studied per se. In this scenario, MoMu — the Fashion Museum of the Province of Antwerp, represents an interesting example. Since its foundation in 2002, MoMu has methodically collected, conserved and exhibited these media materials. This is probably due to its mission of collecting the work of contemporary Belgian designers who have always paid special attention to such communication materials, especially because of their common choice of not advertising.[1] Hence the fact that *Couture Graphique* reports numerous examples of invitations and catalogues by Belgian designers, from Walter Van Beirendonck to Margiela.

By looking at these fashion media materials, this article does not simply offer the opportunity to describe or admire some extravagant fashion objects, but it also aims to propose a critical discourse on these materials in order to reveal the meanings of a fundamental fashion praxis.

FASHION CATALOGUES AS VEHICLES FOR IDEAS

In the catalogue of the exhibition *Yohji Yamamoto* which was held at the Victoria & Albert Museum (2011), art director Marc Ascoli, photographer Nick Knight and graphic designer Peter Saville discussed with writer Magda Keaney, their joint collaboration in the creation of Yamamoto's fashion catalogues. When asked about these promotional materials, Ascoli and Saville vehemently replied: "The lookbook does not exist. They are catalogues and they are purely vehicles of ideas." If the rejection of the commercial attitude of a lookbook can sound more like a need to construct an allure for these 'texts', it is also a way to recall the uniqueness of Yamamoto's catalogue in a scenario that, at the time, perceived such materials merely as trade catalogues for buyers or members of the press. Indeed, the groundbreaking collaboration to produce Yamamoto's catalogues represented a fundamental milestone, not only in the creation of these commercial devices, but also more generally in the affirmation of the fashion image as a transmitter of meaning. This collaborative image of fashion indeed required diverse and shared views: from the photography of Knight to Saville's graphics and Ascoli's direction. As Saville affirms, Yamamoto's catalogue became a melting pot which distilled the essence of the Japanese designer's vision. Saville defines it as the 'Year Zero' and, to some extent, Yamamoto's example represented a sort of new beginning for fashion communication, and also for a new practice of creating fashion catalogues.[2] However, Yamamoto does not represent an isolated phenomenon, since many other Japanese, and also British or Belgian, designers have approached these media materials creatively.

1 Another important aspect arises from MoMu's proximity to the fashion industry. Since it opened in 2002, MoMu's contemporary collection has been built on three private archives which belonged to three founders of the museum, who were also the founders of the Flanders Fashion Institute and, most importantly, three 'fashion insiders': Linda Loppa (the museum's director), Gerdi Esch and Geert Bruloot. The nature of their archives mirrored their experience in the field and, indeed, media materials did form a huge part of these private collections.

2 As I expressly stated above, the collaboration between artists and fashion designers in the production of these media materials is not a recent phenomenon. The history of fashion is full of diverse collaborations: from Madeleine Vionnet and the futurist artist Thayat to Prada and Anna Piaggi. Therefore I do not completely agree with Saville's definition here, since the creation of Yamamoto's catalogues did not represent a brand new phenomenon. However, it must still be recognised that this collaboration did represent a crucial moment in the history of the creation of fashion's image.

In the atlas of Belgian designers especially, we can find multiple approaches to fashion catalogues. While Walter Van Beirendonck has produced comics to present his narratives and contemporaneously portray his creations, Dries Van Noten often uses the catalogues as reports of his fashion show by creating a sort of diary of the event. Although catalogues may vary in shape and layout from collection to collection, some designers adopt a methodical approach to this communicational device, using a specific method to present their creations, collection after collection. Ann Demeulemeester, for example, creates 25 x 20cm books using the same graphical layout each time, with the catalogues always presenting their collections in catwalk pictures. Demeulemeester differentiates only between womenswear and menswear catalogues; reflecting the designer's obsession with black and white, Demeulemeester associates a white cover with menswear, while the womenswear catalogues are always published with a black cover. Another interesting example of such a methodical use of the catalogue is Maison Martin Margiela, who always creates accordion catalogues which seem to resemble Ed Ruscha's art books. Once unfolded, Margiela's catalogues present the collections in images portraying models whose eyes are often obscured by a black blindfold. Furthermore, models are always photographed against the background of a roll of photographic film, and there is always a description of the garment, materials and colours at the side of the picture. This 'Margelian' image has become a distinctive trait of the Maison. A symbolic example of this relevance may be observed in Margiela's menswear S/S 2009 fashion show which consisted of a life-size catalogue.

Such a use of the catalogue testifies how these media materials are not simply utilitarian materials but spaces for the affirmation of designers' ideas — they are vehicles of ideas. Furthermore, catalogues can actually help to shape or evolve designers' ideas, becoming spaces for creation rather than merely affirmation. This is the case with the German designer Bernhard Willhelm who collaborates with the Dutch duo Freudenthal/Verhagen on his catalogues to create Willhelm's burlesque universe. As Jay Hess and Simone Pasztorek report in *Graphic Design for Fashion*, Willhelm encouraged the Dutch duo of designers to interpret his collections and 'produce print-extensions of his garments'.[3] A clear example is the S/S 2007 catalogue which introduced Willhelm's creations into an interactive realm where computer screens and keyboards melded with models and clothes. This particular work by Freudenthal and Verhagen became so central in the work of the designer that, on the occasion of Bernhard Willhelm's retrospective exhibition held at MoMu, the catalogue's image was recreated in 3D. While, on the one hand, all these examples show how the practice of creating catalogues has altered in the last thirty years,[4] on the other they also clearly illustrate the collaborative nature of contemporary fashion.

THE PERFORMATIVITY OF THE FASHION INVITATION

Judith Clark's article entitled 'A Note: Getting the Invitation' addresses the role of fashion invitations in contemporary fashion. Clark opens up a discourse on these materials, highlighting how they are no longer perceived merely as

3 Jay Hess, Simone Pasztorek, *Graphic Design for Fashion*. Laurence King London 2010, p. 158.

4 A discussion of the modifications in these practices has been initiated by Tamsin Blanchard's *Fashion & Graphics* (2004) and by the recent *Graphic Design for Fashion* by Jay Hess and Simone Pasztorek (2010).

Comic strip *King Kong Kooks* by Walter Van Beirendonck, S/S 1989, illustrated by Jan Bosschaert

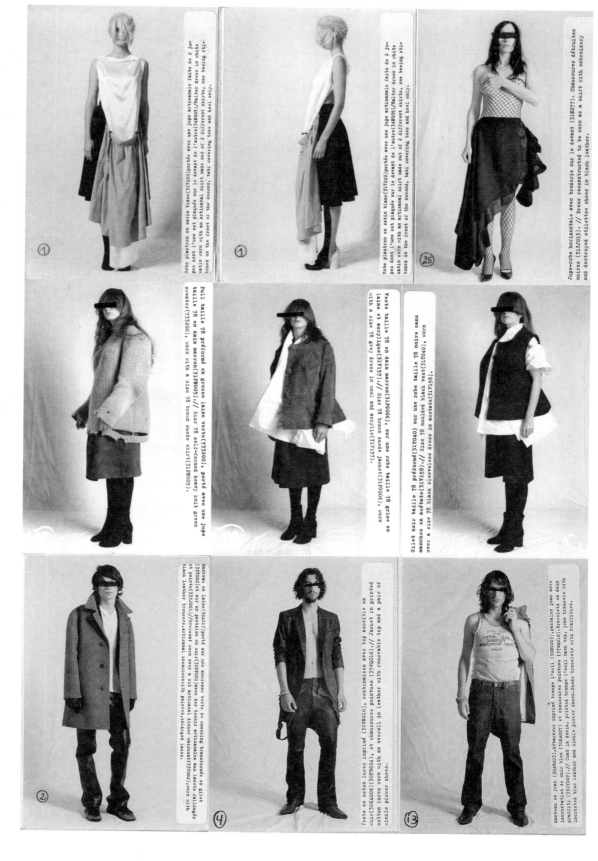

Jupe-robe horizontale avec broderie sur le devant (31E277). Chaussures détruites noires (31E20015). // Dress reconstructed to be worn as a skirt with embroidery and

Robe plastron en satin blanc(31V260)portée avec une jupe artisanale faite de 2 jupes dont l'une est plaquée sur le devant de l'autre(14B005)/Halter dress in white satin worn with an artisanal skirt made out of 2 different skirts, one being stitched on the front of the second, tabi covering toes and heel only.

-tis Martang une étoira pariadilif 2 ub tos tibat tibatte/Tue been tow as second the to -eatun ur snare itet(Twej/(5000WC)ivitail de spxshdY,dre eunl,icht noon urival -mf 2 od lettes etnemettis ejue eem ocav epioe(050J4(5)J4oarti ulive ue nolteruof noon

Pull taille 78 préformé en grosse laine verte(7J3200),porté avec une jupe taille 78 en daim marron(31PM005).// Size 78 well-formed heavy knit green sweater(7J3200), worn with a size 78 brown suede skirt(31PM005).

Veste taille 78 en daim marron(31PG006),sur une robe taille 78 grise en laine et acrylique(31V157).// Size 78 brown suede jacket(31PG006), worn with a size 78 gray dress in wool and acrylic(31V157).

Gilet noir taille 78 préformé(31T040) sur une robe taille 78 noire sans manches en acétate(31V158).// Size 78 moulded black vest(31T040), worn over a size 78 black sleeveless dress in acetate(31V158).

Manteau en laine(30AB012)porté sur une ancienne veste de smoking transformée en gilet (35FQ002)et sur un pantalon en cuir(30FP002)avec des tennis artisanales aux lacets rallongés et pointus(35IT007).// Coat in wool(30AB012)/Overcoat worn over a cut artisanal dinner waistcoat(35FQ002),worn with black leather trousers/artisanal sneakers/with plaited,enlarged laces.

Veste en coton lurex imprimé (30BW010), combinaison avec top amovible en cuir(30KA006)(30FP004), et chaussures pointues (37WQ010).// Jacket in printed cotton lurex worn with an overall in leather with removable top and a pair of winkle picker shoes.

Manteau en jean (30AB003),débardeur imprimé trompe l'oeil (30BC005),pantalon jean avec incrustation de cuir bleu (30AA007) et chaussures pointues (37WQ010).Bracelets en daim sérifin/ (35IT009).// Coat in denim, printed trompe l'oeil tank top, jean trousers with incrusted blue leather and winkle picker shoes./Suede bracelets with graffities.

① ① ㉕

⑵ ⑷ ⑬

65

Above: Invitation for Dries Van Noten, menswear A/W 2002–2003
Below: Lookbook for Dries Van Noten, menswear A/W 2011–2012

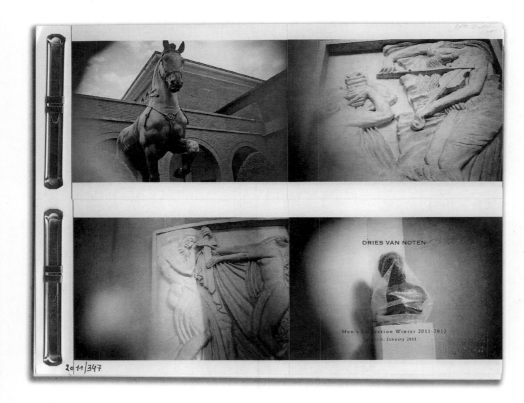

informational devices. Invitations not only communicate when, where, and what designers are showing to the press and buyers, they also carry subliminal messages. According to Clark, the desire for 'getting the invitation' becomes part of the exclusive character of the object, drawing attention to the discourse that the same artefact produces. Indeed, the role of the fashion invitation in contemporary fashion is to make a statement about a collection, a fashion show, an idea. In this sense, fashion invitations are performative objects. Originating in the work of John L. Austin and Judith Butler, the concept of performativity coincides with the concept of an action able to bring into being the condition that the object reiterates. This means that the invitations perform an act in terms of stimulating a relationship with the event for which they are bearing information, namely the fashion show. Although Clark circumscribes these claims to the garments, this allusive character also operates in relation to the show. In fact, many invitations allude to or echo the aesthetic and the contingency of the show.

In some cases, invitations may include direct references to the fashion show, referring to some specific aspects of the event: music, scenography, location or themes. This represents a quite common practice and the exhibition contains several examples, such as Dries Van Noten's menswear A/W 2002–2003 invitation. Designed by the students of the Beaux-Arts of Paris, the invitation resembles the chalk design on the black catwalk. An allusion in reverse is used for the womenswear S/S 2003 invitation, when Van Noten sent a postcard-style invitation portraying a Magritte-like cloud, which was physically reproduced on the ceiling of the fashion show's venue.

While these examples may display a direct relationship to the fashion show, other fashion invitations work in a more allusive register, when invitations resemble the theme or the narrative of the show. This is the case of Maison Martin Margiela's A/W 1998–1999 invitation which took the shape of a concert ticket. The event hosted the visions of the collection by photographer Mark Borthwick, stylist Jane How and writer Sydney Picasso, and the invitation performed this concept through the functionality of the concert ticket. The performativity of the invitation can also be extended to the collection itself. Indeed, the invitation can perform a collection or its principal inspiration, as in the case of A.F. Vandervorst's A/W 2000–2001 invitation: a grey felt sample recalling not only the textile and the colour used for the collection, but also Vandervorst's constant reference to Joseph Beuys's felt metaphors. Another example is Van Noten's S/S 2005 men's invitation: a tiny bottle of scotch within a tweed printed box to resemble the Scottish atmosphere used in his collection. In this sense, the invitation not only announces but becomes part of the fashion show and more broadly of the collection. Its performativity is polysemic and it is expressed through a materiality that, in some cases, is also a mise en scène of its creative process.

Invitation for A.F. Vandevorst by Marc Meulemans, A/W 2000–2001

A controversial example is Jurgi Persoons's A/W 1998–1999 invitation created by the Belgian graphic designer Paul Boudens, one of the most famous 'fashion translators', known for collaborations with famous fashion designers like Yohji Yamamoto, Dries Van Noten and Walter Van Beirendonck. Persoons's invitation was at first sight a common invitation: classic size, stylish font and information about the show. But by opening the invitation, a smear of Boudens's blood became visible. This invitation aimed to represent the dramatic experience of fashion. Indeed, the fashion spectacle does not belong exclusively to the dress or fashion shows, and invitations consciously announce this fact.

'HAUTE COUTURE POETRY': WRITING THE PRESS RELEASE

Written to publicise the collection, the press release is a text that promotes and informs the press and buyers on the forthcoming collection. Commonly, a fashion press release reports the characteristics of the collection, presenting the shapes, colours, materials or inspirations used by designers. According to Olivier Saillard's article entitled 'Mot-ifs – Before and After the Garment: the text' (2007), this practice was systematised at the beginning of the last century, although it is difficult to identify a precise moment when designers began to present their collections through words. In his *The Allure of Chanel* (2009), Paul Morand reports how Chanel began writing a description of the collection in order to give precise information on her work. As with the invitation and the catalogue, the press release was born for specific utilitarian purposes: to present in words the seasonal collection to the press and buyers. As in the case of the invitation and catalogues, this practice has lately assumed diverse variations, becoming a new territory for experimentation that has taken on many different shapes.

Some designers take a methodical approach to the fashion press release, composing a precise description of the materials, inspirations and sartorial techniques used for the collection. In many cases, a description of the show is included. In this sense, the press release becomes an important informational tool. Maison Martin Margiela represents one of the most maniacal approaches to this device. The fashion house's press releases are always divided into three parts. The first (under the heading 'Presentation') and third sections are dedicated to a detailed and precise description of the location, the performance and credits of the show. The second section is called 'Collection' and it presents the Belgian house's various lines, explaining the materials, lines and shapes created for the season. This section, for example, also contains the complete and official description of the numerology of Maison Martin Margiela, thus transforming the press release into a fashion manifesto.

In contrast to such methodical representations, we can also observe less rigid press releases. One of the most interesting examples was born from the collaboration between Anna Piaggi and Prada during the Nineties. Piaggi's fashion writing is unique and aims to express the sound and the look of fashion through the medium of words. In a sort of onomatopoeic practice, Prada's S/S 1998 press releases consisted of assemblages of small poems entitled *Positive Movement, New Detailoring, Positive References*. Verses of these fashion writings include: "Avant-garde work ethic / Sewing machines go crazy / Irons become undisciplined / Nervous are the scissors", and "Positive movement / Of detailing / Of unexpected finishing / Of embroidered seaming [...]". This is not an isolated case, and numerous fashion designers have adopted this free-form style of press release. Raf Simon's press release for his collection

Above and right:
Invitation for Jurgi Persoons by
Paul Boudens, A/W 1998–1999

68

JURGI PERSOONS

You are Cordially invited to the Viewing of
Jurgi Persoons Women's Collection Winter 1998-1999
from 9 until 17 March 1998 at Galerie Bruno Delarue
12, Rue de Thorigny 75003 Paris France

For appointments in advance please contact our Antwerp Office: 0032-3-237 02 05

Jurgi Persoons   Galerie Bruno Delarue
Robert Molsstraat 30 2018 Antwerp Belgium   12, Rue de Thorigny 75003 Paris France
Tel: 0032-3-237 02 05   Fax: 0032-3-238 56 30   Tel: 0033-1-42 78 14 26   Fax: 0033-1-42 78 38 21

Material Worlds (There's no path to follow) took the form of an essay, reflecting on a contemporary ideology of the fashion designer without any reference to the fabric or colours used in the production. For his S/S 2003 collection, the German designer Bernhard Willhelm presented his work through verses such as: "Big Japan / The sun never sets on our happy empire / Beauty without irony / A new idea based on an old truth / So much has been swept under the rug". Whatever their merits may be as poetry, these press releases do achieve their unique aim of translating fashion creations into words.

Despite this heterogeneity, press releases have one common trait: they, as written statements, are always acting as an invitation to imagine the collection (or a fashion show). Such an imaginative characteristic resides in a specific form of description that, as Paola Catenaccio argues in her article 'Press Releases as a Hybrid Genre' (2008), combines promotion and information. In this sense, the press release represents a particular type of description which relies less on authenticity and more on self-representation. Press releases are all 'issued' by fashion brands that, by doing so, testify to a conscious use of this documentary activity that does not simply explain the collection, but also represents a fashion house's ideology. In *The Allure of Chanel* (2009), Paul Morand reports an interesting neologism by Coco Chanel that may be used as an appropriate definition for this category of fashion press releases. The French couturier coined the expression 'haute couture poetry' for a fashion trend that led many designers to conceptualise the names of their fashion creations. In contraposition to this trend, Chanel decided to name her creation with a number — her most famous example being *Chanel No. 5*. With the phrase 'haute couture poetry', Chanel aimed to describe a trend of her time that saw designers writing the text of press releases themselves. Despite her critical viewpoint, Chanel actually invented an interesting neologism that has surfaced of late in a peculiar art of writing the fashion press release.

'ZONES-IN-BETWEEN'

Following the presentation of these practices of fashion communication, the creation of catalogues, invitations and press releases can be perceived as a suitable dimension to observe a practice that embodies designers' ideas beyond the dress. Here, these communicational materials are perceived as spaces of expression rather than mere strategic objects which are prepared by designers' agencies. On the one hand, they fulfil their commercial duty, and on the other they become important dimensions for translating designers' ideas, thanks to the interaction between other disciplines. The art theorist Mieke Bal speaks of 'intermedial translation' to explain translation as an act of moving between gaps, between languages and between disciplines. In this sense, the creation of these communicational materials moves within the gaps between fashion, graphic design, art, fashion writing, etcetera, and within spaces of intersection: 'zones-in-between'. Here, contemporary disciplines meet and interact in order to facilitate the translation of ideas, in a Lyotard-like post-modernist action. For example, the shades of black by Yamamoto and the explosions of colours by Luciano Castelli melt together in a catalogue that aims to represent an idea rather than present a collection. To some extent, communicational materials become materialisations of these encounters,

MAISON MARTIN MARGIELA
Défilé P/E 2007
Dimanche 01 Octobre 2006 à 19h30
2

Invitation for Maison Martin Margiela, S/S 2007

a sort of creative communion where creators, on a micro level, and disciplines, on a macro level, fuse together dialectically. These dialectical encounters, originating in the 'zones-in-between', give birth to new forms of practice that expand the possibilities of fashion.

Today, the abiding issue no longer concerns the question 'When is fashion art?'. On the contrary, the issue, or line of enquiry, coincides with the observation of the dialogues rather than of their limits. It consists in a contextualism that enables the specificity of a practice that manifests itself in the object. In their capacity of being physically attributed to one discipline or another, objects like invitations, catalogues or press releases become detectors of a fashion praxis and, for this reason, they attract our attention.

BIBLIOGRAPHY

Ascoli, Marc, Keaney, Magda, Knight, Nick and Saville, Peter, 'In Conversation. About Yohji Yamamoto' in Ligaya Salazar. *Yohji Yamamoto*. Catalogue of the exhibition *Yohji Yamamoto at the V&A* (12/03/2011-10/07/2011), Abrams Publisher, London 2011.

Bal, Mieke, 'Translating Translation' in *Journal of Visual Culture*, 6(1), 2007, pp. 109–124.

Catenaccio, Paola, 'Press Releases as a Hybrid Genre: Addressing the Informative/Promotional Conundrum' in *Pragmatics*, 18(1), 2008, pp. 9–31.

Clark, Judith, 'A Note: Getting an Invitation', in *Fashion Theory: The Journal of Dress, Body and Culture*, 5(3), 2001, pp. 343–353.

Hess, Jay and Pasztorek, Simone, *Graphic Design for Fashion*, Laurence King Publisher London 2010.

Saillard, Olivier, 'Mot-ifs – Before and after the Garment: the text' in Luca Marchetti, Emmanuele Quinz, *Dysfashional*, catalogue of the exhibition *Dysfashional*, Rotunda, Luxemburg 2007.

Troy, Nancy, *Couture Culture: a Study in Modern Art and Fashion*, MIT Press, Cambridge 2002.

Art director Fabien Baron (1959) has an impressive list of fashion-industry clients. Having studied at the École des Arts Appliqués in Paris from 1975 to 1976, Baron started his career with French newspaper *L'Équipe*. In 1982, he moved to New York to work for the magazines *Self*, *GQ* and *Woman*. From the late Eighties onwards, he was in great demand, and became art director for high-end department store Barney's and the Italian edition of *Vogue*. Many more fashion magazines followed in subsequent years, including *Interview* (1990), *Harper's Bazaar* (1992), *Arena Homme +* (from 2000 to 2002, with Baron working as chief editor in addition to creative director) and *Vogue Paris* (from 2003 to 2008). Since 2008, Fabien Baron has been working for *Interview* once again, this time as editorial director.

Fabien Baron founded the creative agency Baron & Baron in 1990, which went on to develop advertising campaigns for fashion labels such as Issey Miyake, Hugo Boss, Giorgio Armani, Valentino, Pucci, Michael Kors, Norma Kamali, Balenciaga, Burberry and Miu Miu. His most loyal customer is Calvin Klein, and he has been in charge of art direction for the company's promotional campaigns since 1992. Baron's campaign for Calvin Klein's *Obsession* perfume in the early Nineties brought not only worldwide fame but also controversy. Under Baron's direction, photographer Mario Sorrenti captured his then-girlfriend Kate Moss, childlike, emaciated and naked, in an androgynous shot. The campaign typifies Baron's moderate and sparing style: he likes to leave the occasional page blank, and uses classic fonts such as Didot, Futura or Bodoni. He applied similar techniques when working as art director on the groundbreaking book *Sex* (1992) by Madonna, for instance. Fabien Baron's style is often compared to that of Alexey Brodovitch (1898–1971), who was art director for fashion magazine *Harper's Bazaar* from 1934 to 1958. He too was a fan of Didot, left pages blank, and took great care to make sure that the magazine's layout brought out the best in the photography.

www.baron-baron.com

CK Calvin Klein Jeans advertisement, A/W 1993–1994

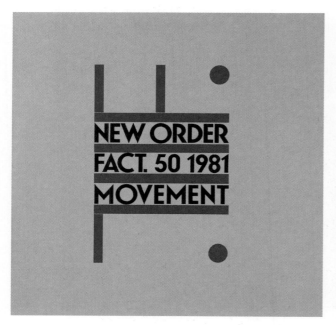

Top: Yohji Yamamoto advertisement, *Game Over*, A/W 1991–1992
Bottom: *Movement* (1981), *Power, Corruption & Lies* (1983), *Technique* (1989), album covers designed by Peter Saville for the band New Order

After graduating from Manchester Polytechnic in 1978, graphic designer Peter Saville (1955) immediately started working for the independent recording label Factory Records, which he also co-founded. The album covers that Saville designed for bands such as Joy Division, New Order and Orchestral Manoeuvres In The Dark became famous around the world. Initially, Saville drew much of his inspiration from modernistic symbolism — he called Herbert Spencer's book *Pioneers of Modern Typography* his Bible — but from the early Eighties onwards, he increasingly incorporated references to classic art in his work. For the sleeve of New Order's album *Power, Corruption and Lies* (1983), for example, Saville juxtaposed a painting of a basket of roses by Henri Fantin-Latour with a colour-coded alphabet. The use of one genre to place another genre, in this case classic art history, in a new context became one of the hallmarks of Saville's work.

In 1986, Peter Saville worked with art director Marc Ascoli and photographer Nick Knight to develop an advertising campaign and lookbook for Japanese designer Yohji Yamamoto. The trio created a series of images, of which the most famous is a silhouette-like shot of Naomi Campbell wearing a red bustle — this has since gone down in fashion history as a groundbreaking image. Saville himself refers to this colla-boration as 'Year Zero': the start of his minimalistic approach in which he based his designs only on the absolute necessities. Saville went on to develop several more campaigns for Yamamoto which were less popular, particularly among Yamamoto's distributors. For a series of advertisements in 1991, Saville used stock photos rather than images of the designs themselves, accompanied by slogans such as 'Game over'. The ads illustrated how both Saville and Yamamoto felt about the fashion industry at that time, namely that it was facing a creative crisis.

Saville also worked for other designers including Jil Sander, Martine Sitbon, John Galliano, Christian Dior and Stella McCartney. In 2000, together with photographer Nick Knight, Saville launched the website SHOWstudio, a platform with the aim of exploring the boundaries limiting the online promotion of fashion. The website still exists today and is mainly focused on creating short fashion films, although Peter Saville is no longer involved with it.

In 2003, Peter Saville allowed fashion designer Raf Simons, a great admirer of Saville, access to his archives. For garments in his Autumn/Winter 2003–2004 menswear collection, Simons used designs from Saville's Factory Records period as prints.

www.petersaville.com

The M/M (Paris) creative agency was founded in 1992 by Mathias Augustyniak (1967) and Michael Amzalag (1968). The pair met in 1988 while at the École Nationale Supérieure des Arts Décoratifs. Amzalag left in 1990 and joined the music magazine *Les Inrockuptibles* as art director, and Augustyniak decided to switch to studying at the Royal College of Art in London, from where he graduated in 1991. The first of M/M (Paris)'s clients came mainly from the music industry. The duo designed album covers for little-known French singers such as Silvain Vanot and Mathilda May.

In 1993, the duo embarked on a project for Y's, the new line from fashion designer Yohji Yamamoto. More clients from the world of fashion followed, including Jil Sander and Martine Sitbon, and later Stella McCartney, A.P.C. and Givenchy. The pair also spent several years in charge of art direction for a number of magazines, including *Vogue Paris* (from 2001 to 2003), *Arena Homme +* (from 2007 to 2009) and *Interview* (in 2009).

In 1995, the M/M (Paris) gentlemen met photography duo Inez van Lamsweerde & Vinoodh Matadin, which resulted in numerous joint projects. Their advertisements for the French fashion house Balenciaga, such as for the Summer and Winter collections of 2001, were particularly iconic; the style with which M/M (Paris) decorated the photos by Van Lamsweerde & Matadin with expressive, hand-drawn illustrations has since become their trademark. In the campaign for the S/S 2001 collection, for example, coloured pencils were used to draw a bird on the shoulders and forehead of the model Delfine Bafort, and in the campaign for the A/W 2001–2002 collection, Christy Turlington appeared, on an otherwise deserted basketball court, under attack by a dripping image of her own head.

In 2002, M/M (Paris) handled the art direction for American fashion label Calvin Klein's jeans advertisements. On raggedly cut out black-and-white photos by Inez van Lamsweerde & Vinoodh Matadin, M/M (Paris) drew the label's logo in the characteristic Calvin Klein font using red and blue pens. In addition to advertising campaigns, the foursome collaborated on a number of freestyle projects including 'The Alphabet' (2001) and 'The Alphamen' (2003), both of which appeared in *V Magazine*. For these two projects, M/M (Paris) created a typography from the portrait shots Van Lamsweerde and Matadin had taken of various models.

Meanwhile, M/M Paris has not completely turned its back on the music industry. Since 2001, the duo — yet again with Inez van Lamsweerde & Vinoodh Matadin – has been working regularly with Icelandic singer Björk. The fruits of their collaboration include the artwork for her albums *Vespertine* (2001) and *Biophilia* (2011).

www.mmparis.com

Left: invitation for Balenciaga by Inez van Lamsweerde & Vinoodh Matadin and M/M (Paris), 2002
Right: Balenciaga advertisement by Inez van Lamsweerde & Vinoodh Matadin and M/M (Paris), S/S 2001

Above: *Christy (Enhanced)*, Inez van Lamsweerde & Vinoodh Matadin
and M/M (Paris), 2002
Below left: A.P.C. advertisement by Inez van Lamsweerde & Vinoodh Matadin
and M/M (Paris), A/W 2009/2010
Right: *Love You (Mon amour m'a baisé)*, 2005

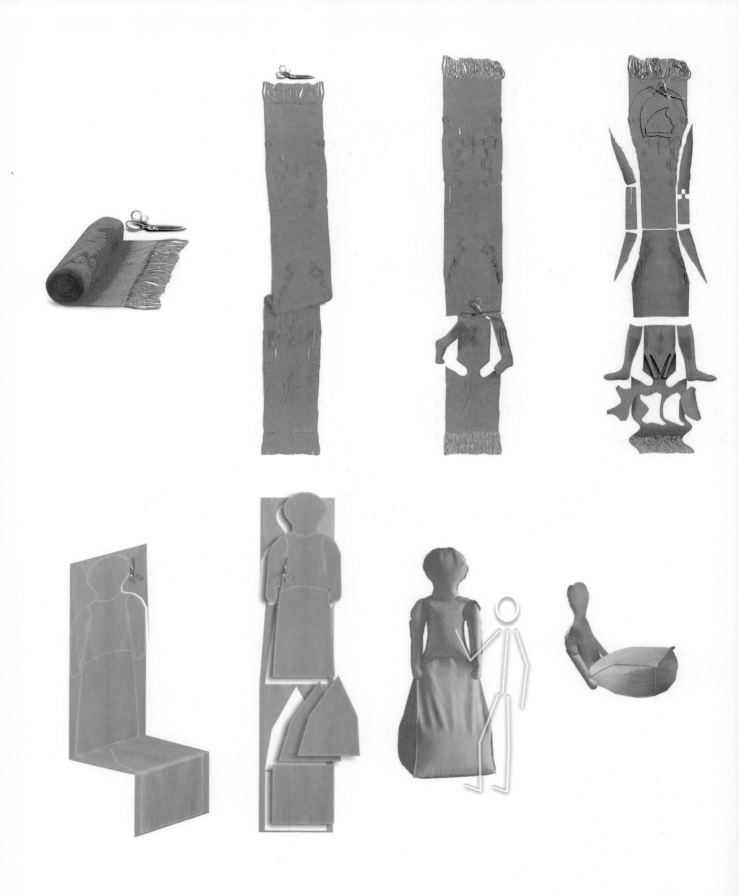

Above: A-POC *Queen*, 1998
Below: A-POC *Midas*, 2000
Right: A-POC animation logo by Pascal Roulin

In 1998, Japanese fashion designer Issey Miyake (1938) and his design partner Dai Fujiwara (1967, Design Engineer for A-POC, Creative Director for ISSEY MIYAKE 2006–2011) launched the A-POC label (an acronym of 'A Piece of Cloth'). A-POC signified Miyake's desire to find new ways of making clothing that addressed both the demands of a modern lifestyle and the constraints of our world. The earliest evolution of the technique which harnessed computer technology to an industrial knitting machine (later expanded to a weaving machine) created fabric, texture and the components of a fully finished garment in a single process. The knits appealed to the idea of mass-produced clothing that could be customised. However, Miyake, never one to rest with a single idea, moved away from that to further explore the technique as it could be applied to create a textile, texture and the components for clothing in a single process using computer technology.

Miyake knew that for this new way of making clothes, he would need a new way to explain the process. He approached Belgian film director and designer Pascal Roulin (1958), whose animations and whimsical graphics would serve as the visual explanation for the continuing evolution of the A-POC process. Roulin initially developed a series of fourteen short films demonstrating A-POC's production process from start to finish for the 'Issey Miyake Making Things' exhibition at Fondation Cartier pour l'Art Contemporain in Paris in 1998. Miyake was so delighted by their simplicity, clarity and sense of fun that he has used Roulin's work for all A-POC promotions ever since, including a looping visual of the logo which was also created by Roulin. It embodied everything that A-POC stood for: intelligent design, fun and creativity.

Pascal Roulin sketched out his animations using a rough storyboard format. The technique started using photos that he then retouched and morphed as with stop-motion animation. He also used computer graphics to depict a flat piece of cloth being unrolled before becoming the outfit. As his collaboration with Midori Kitamura evolved, he included storyboard-like, hand-drawn pictures which she found both whimsical and easy to comprehend.

www.mds.isseymiyake.com

Carmen Freudenthal (1965) and Elle Verhagen (1962) met in the early Eighties while they were both studying at the Gerrit Rietveld Academie in Amsterdam, and they've been working together since 1989. Photography, styling, graphic design — Freudenthal/Verhagen have done it all and more. In their own recognisably quirky and humoristic style, they have been featured in magazines such as i-D, Dazed & Confused, Jalouse, Flash Art International and Blend, and have designed advertising campaigns for brands including Absolut Vodka, Fatboy, de Bijenkorf and citizenM hotels.

From 2001 to 2007, Freudenthal/Verhagen played a significant role in shaping the visual identity of German fashion designer Bernhard Willhelm (1972). Having been introduced to each other by mutual friend and stylist Maarten Spruyt, Freudenthal/Verhagen's visual language turned out to be an excellent match for Willhelm's colourful, extravagant and slightly hysterical designs. The duo made catalogues, a few short fashion films and a book celebrating the 5th anniversary of the Bernhard Willhelm label. In their first project for him, the catalogue for his S/S 2001 collection, they drew inspiration from a cookery book and put it together by hand. At a time when many photographers were starting to experiment with a new kind of computer software called Photoshop, Freudenthal/Verhagen reached for the scissors and snipped away at a discarded IKEA catalogue to produce a collage-style catalogue. While they switched to Photoshop shortly afterwards, they still make many of the props for their shoots by hand — it typifies the Freudenthal/Verhagen approach. The duo uses and abuses modern-day visual language and photographic techniques to create an unmistakable style. It was due to this humoristic approach to everyday life, and the way they blurred the boundaries between reality and fiction, that Bernhard Willhelm decided to give Freudenthal/Verhagen complete artistic freedom for every project. The result was a lively collection of catalogues, short fashion films and a book. For the S/S 2006 collection, Freudenthal/Verhagen designed A1-sized catalogues showing photographs of a naked Bernhard and his right-hand woman Jutta Kraus being attacked by mean fashion fairies. The short film the duo made for Willhelm for his S/S 2007 collection, 'The Singing Girls', was particularly striking. Film footage of faces singing a folk song was overlaid onto a photo of a group of young girls. The effect was magical and macabre in equal measure.

Having worked for Bernhard Willhelm for seven years, Freudenthal and Verhagen agreed it was time to stop — things had got too much for them. At the time of compiling the book for the Bernhard Willhelm label's 5th anniversary, they were dedicating eight months out of a twelve-month period entirely to his projects. As Carmen Freudenthal put it, "You have to watch out that you don't turn into Bernhard Willhelm." Meanwhile, due to the growth of the internet, catalogues were beginning to lose their importance for presenting new collections to fashion journalists, stylists and buyers. Nowadays, websites like style.com and nowfashion.com, and social media channels such as Twitter and Facebook offer people almost instant access to the latest collections, thus rendering catalogues obsolete.

In addition to their projects for Bernhard Willhelm, Freudenthal/Verhagen also worked for a number of other fashion designers. They made a short fashion film for Saskia van Drimmelen's 'Painted Series', for instance, in which invisible hands dressed a young girl for an evening out. In the summer of 2011, Freudenthal/Verhagen also produced a short film called 'Dear Mr/Mrs' featuring the graduation collections of students from the ArtEZ Fashion Masters programme.

www.freudenthalverhagen.com

Top: Catalogue for Bernhard Willhelm, womenswear S/S 2006
Bottom: Catalogue for Bernhard Willhelm, menswear S/S 2005

Catalogue for Bernhard Willhelm, womenswear S/S 2005

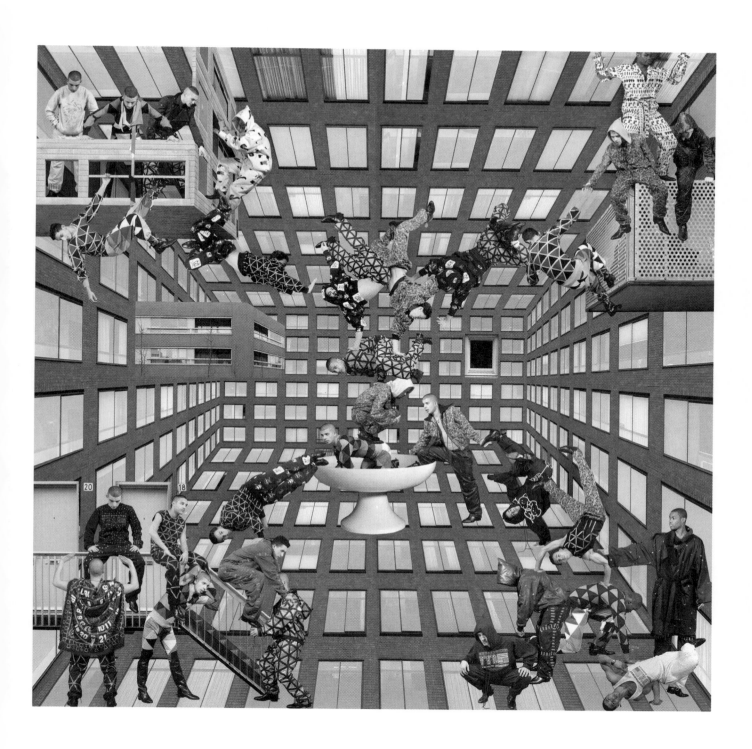

Catalogue for Bernhard Willhelm, menswear A/W 2003–2004

JURGI PERSOONS
WOMEN'S COLLECTION
WINTER
1999-2000

FROM 5 UNTIL 16 MARCH
AT GALERIE BRUNO DELARGE
12 RUE DE THORIGNY
75003 PARIS
TEL: 33 1 42 78 08 21 4
FAX: 33 1 42 78 14 26
FOR ALL APPOINTMENTS PLEASE
CONTACT OUR ANTWERP OFFICE
TEL: 32 3 3
FAX:

Although Paul Boudens (1965) initially moved to Antwerp to study fashion, he ended up — after several detours via courses in communications and interpreting/translating — in the graphic design department of the 'Sint-Lucas Paviljoen'. Having spotted Boudens's self-made postcards and sleeves for audio cassettes at a birthday party, a lecturer told him that he should study for a degree in graphic design — and so he did. In his third year, around 1988, Paul Boudens did some work for Walter Van Beirendonck, who was just on the verge of his breakthrough with the 'Antwerp Six'. After graduating, Boudens continued to worked as a freelancer for Van Beirendonck. And because Antwerp is a relatively small city with an even smaller fashion scene, he enjoyed a snowball effect: Paul Boudens's customer base had soon expanded to include the likes of Wim Neels, Jurgi Persoons, A.F. Vandevorst, Olivier Theyskens, Haider Ackermann and Yohji Yamamoto. Since then, Boudens has designed for Antwerp's Royal Academy of Fine Arts, the MoMu Fashion Museum, the Rosas dance group, and theatre company Het Zuidelijk Toneel. In addition, 2001 saw him co-launch *[N°] A Magazine*. For each edition, a different fashion designer was allowed free rein to fill the magazine with whatever inspired them, while Boudens took care of the graphics.

Paul Boudens likes to work with his hands. This probably stems from his time at school, where there was just one computer. Not prepared to waste time hanging around waiting to use it, Boudens instead set to work with a typewriter and a silk-screen printing machine. While there's no shortage of computers nowadays, he still prefers a hands-on approach, and his love of craftsmanship resonates through his designs. For Jurgi Persoons, Boudens splattered invitations with blood and made an ingenious, interwoven creation of wire and nails. When Olivier Theyskens asked him to 'ruin' his name, Paul Boudens designed invitations on which the Theyskens name had been scratched out by hand.

Another designer for whom Boudens has played around with the theme of imperfection is Yohji Yamamoto. When Boudens began work for the label in 2003, the company had very limited funds, partly due to spending heavily on expensive catalogues and advertising campaigns created by his predecessors, M/M (Paris). But the budgetary restrictions served only to spur him on creatively, as demonstrated by the invitations he designed: printed on both sides, splashed with red paint, stitched by hand and decorated with stickers. His aim was always to lend his invitations a handmade feel, as if each one had been specially created for the invitee.

This personal touch can be found in the invitations he designed for Haider Ackermann too. With Boudens's very first invitation for Ackermann, he established a standard format based on a thick, rectangular piece of card that fit into a regular envelope. He would subsequently change it each season by altering the colour, material and typography. Boudens also created a sort of 'Haider Ackermann-handwriting' every season, sometimes just for his signature and other times for the entire text. The colours of the invitations are inspired by the colours used in Ackermann's own designs, which are subtle and restrained — a different angle for Boudens, who is a big fan of colour, especially red. In addition to his invitation designs, he also created a small booklet, full of Ackermann's sources of inspiration, to accompany the only menswear collection Haider Ackermann ever designed, namely for the occasion of Pitti Uomo 2010.

Why do designers enjoy working with Boudens so much? As he himself says, "I can get inside fashion designers' heads, I understand their world. I'm probably slightly schizophrenic."

www.a-g-i.org/paulboudens

Left: invitation for Jurgi Persoons, A/W 1999–2000
Below: *N°A Magazine*, 2001

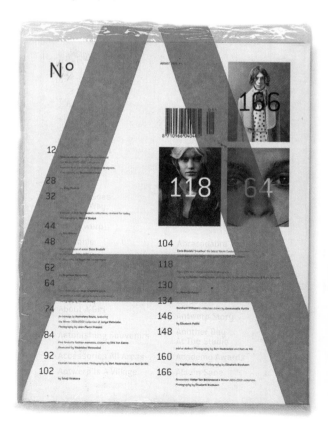

Above: invitations for Yohji Yamamoto, S/S 2005
Right: invitations for Yohji Yamamoto, S/S 2004
Below: invitations for Y's Yohji Yamamoto, A/W 2003–2004
invitations for Yohji Yamamoto, A/W 2003–2004

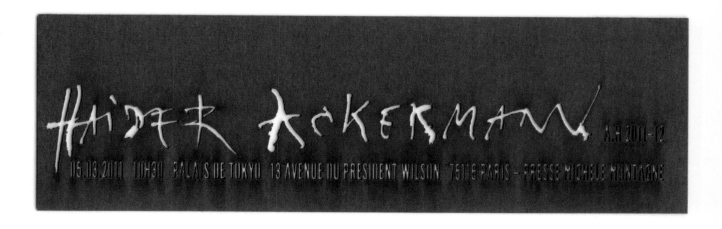

Top: invitation for Olivier Theyskens, A/W 1999–2000
Bottom: invitation for Haider Ackermann, A/W 2011–2012

Armand Mevis (1963) and Linda van Deursen (1961) met while they were both studying graphic design at the Gerrit Rietveld Academie in Amsterdam. Since the idea of working for a design agency after graduation left them both cold, they decided to go it alone, together. One of their first projects was designing a catalogue to accompany an exhibition at the Fonds BKVB (The Netherlands Foundation for Visual Arts, Design and Architecture) in 1993, celebrating the foundation's first five years (1988–1992). The catalogue, called 'De Kracht van Heden', soon led to a stream of projects from other cultural institutions. Since the work of Mevis & Van Deursen was so different from what the major design studios such as Studio Dumbar, Total Design and Hard Werken were doing, they soon made their name in the graphic design world. With their recognisably pared back — almost severe — style, Mevis & Van Deursen regarded graphic design not merely as a vehicle for communication, but also as an active component of the message itself. Their approach enabled them to secure poster-designing projects for The Amsterdam Music Theatre, for instance, and for numerous exhibitions. They also created the house style for several big names in the cultural world, including Museum Boijmans Van Beuningen, Stedelijk Museum Bureau Amsterdam (SMBA) and the art magazine *Metropolis M*, and designed the layout of many books on art.

1997 marked the start of Mevis & Van Deursen's first project for fashion designers Viktor & Rolf. Their brief was to create an invitation for *Le Regard Noir*, an exhibition to be held in the SMBA, and they also developed the exhibition catalogue. The collaboration was a success, resulting in Mevis & Van Deursen being asked to design the invitation for Viktor & Rolf's first couture show in Paris in early 1998. Because couture is intended for only a select group of people, it was not deemed necessary to design an official logo for the fashion house itself at that time. However, that changed in 2000 when Viktor & Rolf branched out into designing and presenting prêt-à-porter. Mevis & Van Deursen developed a logo that reflected Viktor & Rolf's ambition to become a major, classic fashion house, and which immediately lent the fledgling designers a suitable allure: the wax seal. They were inspired by Salvador Dalí, and in particular by one of his paintings, 'Soft Watch at Moment of First Explosion' from 1954. Mevis & Van Deursen believed that just as Dalí's surrealistic art worked on a subconscious level, so too did fashion — and especially the Viktor & Rolf designs. The wax seal, slightly out of proportion and jet black, contained a hint of fetishism, something all too commonly associated with the fast-paced,

Invitations for Viktor & Rolf, created by students of the Gerrit Rietveld Academie, S/S 2003

consumption-focused fashion world. Fetishism is also a theme that echoes through Viktor & Rolf's own work, mainly because, especially in their early period, they magnified that aspect of the fashion world — partly to poke fun at it, but also because they were so desperately keen to become part of it themselves. Examples include their fake perfume campaign for *Le Parfum* in 1996 and the *L'Apparence du Vide* installation in 1995, which featured young girls' voices chanting the names of the supermodels of the day.

The wax seal made such a good impression on Viktor & Rolf that they adopted it for their house style and lookbooks, and included it as standard in the top-right corner of the A4-sized invitations for their catwalk shows. The seal also regularly features in their designs, including embroidered logos on men's jumpers and shirts, on handbags and luggage, on perfume bottles, on wrapping paper and in decors for their catwalk shows. The invitations that Mevis & Van Deursen designed in collaboration with graphic design students for Viktor & Rolf's S/S 2003 collection were truly unique. Each student was given a blank sheet of standard A4 paper with the seal and told to design an invitation by hand. The result was a colourful and diverse array of one-of-a-kind invitations.

www.mevisvandeursen.nl

invite you to attend the Spring Summer 2005 Show
Wednesday, October 6th at 4.30 pm

Espace Éphémère - Jardin des Tuileries
Grand Bassin de la Concorde
Entrée Grille d'Honneur Concorde
Paris 1er

PRESS EU   KARLA OTTO   T 00331 42 61 34 36   F 00331 42 61 58 91
PRESS US   PR CONSULTING   T 001 212 228 81 81   F 001 212 228 87 87

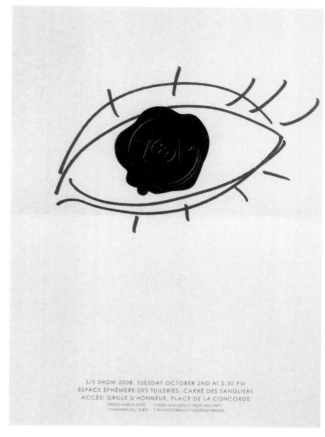

S/S SHOW 2008. TUESDAY OCTOBER 2ND AT 2.30 PM
ESPACE ÉPHÉMÈRE DES TUILERIES, CARRÉ DES SANGLIERS
ACCÈS: GRILLE D'HONNEUR, PLACE DE LA CONCORDE

PRESS/ KARLA OTTO   T 0033142613436/ F 0033142615891
COMMERCIAL/ GIBO   T 0039025748061/ F 0039025748650

Viktor & Rolf invite you to attend
the Fall / Winter 2002 2003 show
Saturday March 9 at 18:30 H
at Studio Gabriel
9, Avenue Gabriel - 75008 Paris

VIKTOR&ROLF
PRESS JE BUREAU SYLVIE GRUMBACH   T 01 42559518 / F 01 40264553
PRESS USA PR CONSULTING   T 212 2288181 / F 212 2288787

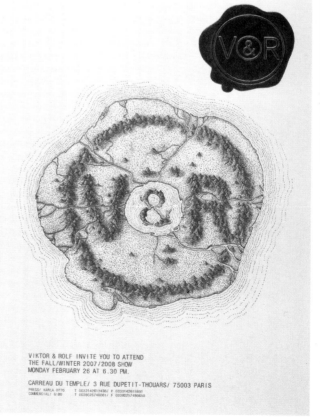

VIKTOR & ROLF INVITE YOU TO ATTEND
THE FALL/WINTER 2007/2008 SHOW
MONDAY FEBRUARY 26 AT 6.30 PM.

CARREAU DU TEMPLE/ 3 RUE DUPETIT-THOUARS/ 75003 PARIS

PRESS/ KARLA OTTO   T 0033142613436/ F 0033142615891
COMMERCIAL/ GIBO   T 0039025748061/ F 0039025748650

Above: invitation for Paul Smith, S/S 2003
Below: invitation for Paul Smith, womenswear S/S 2001

Alan Aboud (1966) has been in charge of graphic design for the Paul Smith label for no less than twenty-three years — a record in the fashion industry. Aboud studied graphic design at the National College of Art & Design in Dublin, before transferring to the Saint Martins School of Art in London from where he graduated in 1989. He immediately joined forces with fellow graduate Sandro Sodano to set up the creative agency Aboud Sodano, which changed its name to Aboud Creative in 2007.

Over the years, Aboud Sadano has worked for various fashion brands, including Levi's, H&M and River Island, but Paul Smith was always the agency's biggest client and remains so to this day. Aboud was scouted by a Smith employee during the presentation of his thesis project at Saint Martins, and shortly afterwards he was designing advertisements and invitations for catwalk shows. Slowly but surely, the number of projects increased, ranging from designing websites, products, store interiors, advertorials and packaging, to labels for in the garments themselves.

The most recognisable details on the Paul Smith label are the hand-written logo and the multicoloured stripes. The basic design for the logo already existed when Aboud started working for Paul Smith in 1989. "It was a friend of his in Nottingham in the 1970s who drew 'Paul Smith' for him — probably on the back of a cigarette packet or something," says Aboud. He simply adapted it slightly, refining it into the logo as it is today. The multicoloured stripes were used for the first time in 1996, on invitations, and then again in 1998, this time on the previously grey bags. "We took inspiration from a textile print in the archive. It was based on the Bridget Riley style of painting. I loved it. Everything we had before was grey, which was a bizarre anomaly for a designer who was so known for his use of colour."[1]

One of the unique things about Paul Smith is his fascination for patterns and motifs, which he collects or photographs. Hence the fact that stripes (and sometimes even cheerful floral prints) often feature in his designs, although he tends to prefer the subtle touch, including them on the reverse of a collar or as the lining. There are two versions of the multicoloured stripes: a straight one for his menswear and a wavy, flowing one for his women's range.

Aboud and Smith have been working in the same manner for the past twenty-three years. As a source of inspiration, Paul Smith takes photographs of country estates, wallpaper, flowers or even dancers performing a ballet — anything that catches his eye. After a little artistic treatment from Aboud, a flower from one of Smith's photos could easily end up as the image for the label's latest perfume. Smith and Aboud are united in their endeavour to create new visual material that is truly unique, and they use literally any element as input to help them do so.

Whether the project in question is a campaign, an invitation, a window display or a perfume, it always fulfils a number of criteria. Firstly, the product or image should be classic but with a twist and/or a hint of humour. Secondly, photos should never be altered or retouched, but instead remain 'true to the material'. Any effects must be created by camera rather than in post-processing, such as in the campaign for which the decision was taken not to photograph the models' heads. Thirdly, 'real' people should be used instead of professional models.

Because the work process itself is so important to the overall brand, the Paul Smith fashion house has regularly produced behind-the-scenes films in recent years, revealing Paul Smith's inspirational world to a wider audience and providing insights into how his products come about.

www.aboud-creative.com

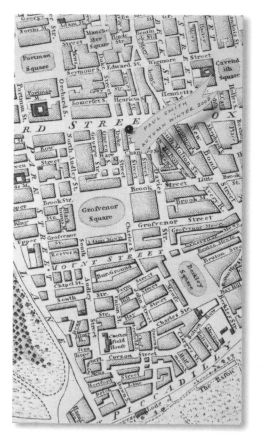

Invitation for Paul Smith, A/W 2008-2009

1 Tamsin Blanchard, *Fashion & Graphics*, Laurence King London 2004, p. 138.

Above: Jil Sander advertisement, photographed by Craig McDean,
art direction by Marc Ascoli, S/S 1996
Right: Catalogue for Yohji Yamamoto, photographed by Paolo Roversi,
art direction by Marc Ascoli, A/W 1985–1986

While Marc Ascoli (1955) has not become as famous as many of the fashion photographers whose careers he helped to launch — such as Nick Knight, Max Vadukul, Craig McDean, Paolo Roversi and Peter Lindbergh — his work as art director has been just as influential, if not more so. From 1984 to 1991, Ascoli was in charge of the advertising campaigns, catalogues and catwalk show designs for Japanese fashion label Yohji Yamamoto. It was in this role, in 1986, that he scouted the then-unknown photographer Nick Knight and graphic designer Peter Saville, and the trio went on to produce a series of groundbreaking campaigns. In addition to his work for Yamamoto, Marc Ascoli developed campaigns for Chloé (1987–1991), Jil Sander (1988–2000), Martine Sitbon (1986 to present), Cerruti, Hugo Boss, Calvin Klein, Iceberg and Emanuel Ungaro. The catalogues he designed for Jil Sander in collaboration with Nick Knight won the award for the best international campaign at the International Festival of Fashion Photography in Barcelona in both 1991 and 1992.

In 2007, Marc Ascoli and his wife, fashion designer Martine Sitbon, joined forces with Japanese investment company Semeiotics, Inc. to set up the Rue du Mail label. Ascoli, in the role of 'image director', regards Rue du Mail as more than just a fashion label — he sees it as a platform for opening up the studio, workshop and boutique to the press, buyers and the general public. Whereas it was the fashion designer who was placed on a pedestal and treated like a king in the Eighties, Ascoli believes that the focus has now shifted to the products themselves. Large-scale, decadent productions for promotional campaigns and catwalk shows are passé; the idea of a designer in an ivory tower, who only puts in an appearance at a collection launch, is outdated. Nowadays, it is essential to have a direct relationship with consumers. Extravagant concept stores have become irrelevant. At the end of the day, all people want is a great-looking jacket, dress or pair of trousers.

www.marcascoli.com

Catalogue for Yohji Yamamoto, photographed by Nick Knight, art direction by Marc Ascoli, A/W 1987–1988

INSCRIBING THE BODY: TEXT, SYMBOLS & THE T-SHIRT

— JOSÉ TEUNISSEN & HANKA VAN DER VOET

Every day, our clothing helps us to communicate our personal identity. A slogan on our T-shirt can even enable us to express our political views publicly, which makes the T-shirt the most 'communicative' garment in the modern-day wardrobe: a symbol of the interface between the body and language, according to Patricia Calefato.[1] This communicative value is at the heart of the T-shirt's continuing popularity, because the garment itself, jersey fabric in a 'T' shape, has hardly changed in the course of the past century. Its neutrality makes it ideal for conveying a message, be it political ideology or the logo of a sports team, university or even a fashion brand. In effect, you are wearing a banner across your chest. The T-shirt is the favourite brand vehicle of many fashion labels from Dior to North Face, while for streetwear and sportswear brands, it is one of the most crucial garments, matched only by the shoe.

The T-shirt's transition to outerwear coincided with the rise of youth culture and pop music in the 1950s. It became trendy around the same time as jeans and they both became symbolic of personal freedom and a casual, informal (fashion) culture. In the Seventies, the T-shirt became strongly asso-ciated with the underground movement and graffiti culture. In this chapter, we will document the T-shirt's journey through youth culture and (graffiti) art to be-coming an indispensable part of communication in contemporary culture.

FROM MILITARY GARMENT TO SPORT SHIRT

It is not precisely clear how and where the first T-shirt was made. One cer-tainty however, is that the army played a key role in the T-shirt's popularity as outerwear. The T-shirt was initially worn as underwear in the mid-nineteenth century, mainly by miners and dockworkers. During the First World War, European soldiers wore T-shirts under their uniforms; the cotton jersey proved to be ideal for absorbing sweat, much to the envy of the American soldiers who had to endure the itchiness of woollen T-shirts. By the time of the Great Depression, the cotton T-shirt had crossed the Atlantic to the USA and become standard attire for agricultural labourers.

1 Patricia Calefato, 'Fashion as sign system', in: Jan Brand and José Teunissen (eds.), *The Power of Fashion. On design and meaning*, p. 140.

The first T-shirt featuring words and numbers was produced for sporting purposes. In 1932, underwear manufacturer Jockey developed an absorbent jersey T-shirt for the USC Trojans American football team. The club added its own logo and printed the players' names and numbers on the back. So the archetypical printed T-shirt dates back to the Thirties, but its fashion break-through had to wait until the Fifties and the emergence of youth culture.

T-SHIRT AS A SYMBOL OF YOUTH CULTURE

The T-shirt's popularity exploded in the Fifties when the singer Elvis Presley chose to wear tight white T-shirts with his jeans, and when the actors Marlon Brando and James Dean wore the same in their leading roles in the films *On the Waterfront* (1954) and *Rebel Without a Cause* (1955) respectively. The three of them symbolised two interesting developments. Firstly, a changing society in which the youth was rebelling against the older generation. With their own musical culture and new style of dress, they distanced themselves from a culture based on status and a class-based hierarchy, and replaced it with a much more individual, democratic and informal lifestyle. The T-shirt (and jeans) has retained that image ever since.

Secondly, the T-shirt marked a move towards the eroticisation of the (male) body.[2] Up until the Sixties, few, if any, items of men's clothing were designed to emphasise the male physique. The suit obscured rather than accentuated a man's body[3] and, similarly, the classic free-time attire of plus fours and tank tops lacked any tight-fitting garments for displaying the male contours. This made the impact of the first T-shirts (with jeans) spectacular: the T-shirt sleeves accentuated Marlon Brando's muscular arms and the thin fabric left little to the imagination about the six-pack beneath. Previously, that game of defining, concealing and revealing had been restricted to the female body, with attention jumping from cleavage to stomach and then to the back.[4] According to Roland Barthes, eroticism starts right where the garment gapes and defines the lines of the body.[5] As a result, Marlon Brando and James Dean became the first male film stars to have a brooding, sexy image.

When words were first printed onto T-shirts in the Sixties, the garment was suddenly asking to be seen. Rather than passers-by having to steal a casual glance, it became acceptable to openly look at it. Hence, reading someone's T-shirt became a permitted way of eyeing up someone's body; reading and allowing it to be read became the first steps in a subtle erotic process. That is how the T-shirt has become one of fashion's most subtle, tantalising garments, especially in menswear, and has remained so ever since.

THE T-SHIRT AS A POLITICAL PAMPHLET

The Sixties marked the start of the T-shirt's role as a vehicle for commercial or political messages. In the run-up to the presidential elections in 1960, John F. Kennedy's campaign team fanatically handed out T-shirts displaying the slogan 'Kennedy for president'. During the Vietnam War, the anti-war movement also distributed T-shirts featuring slogans such as 'Make Love, Not War', 'Draft Beer, Not Boys' and 'Eighteen Today, Dead Tomorrow'. T-shirts printed with

2 Eroticisation of the female body was the norm: clothing would accentuate the legs, the cleavage, the stomach or the shape of the back. Yet the T-shirt brought with it a new variation: the wet T-shirt — a phenomenon made popular by Bo Derek in particular.

3 Anne Hollander, *Sex and Suits.*

4 Eric de Kuyper, *De verbeelding van het mannelijk lichaam*, p. 104.

5 Roland Barthes, *Système de la mode.*

6 Patricia Calefato, 'Fashion as sign system', in: Jan Brand and José Teunissen (eds.), *The Power of Fashion. On design and meaning*, p. 132.

James Dean in *Rebel Without A Cause,* 1955

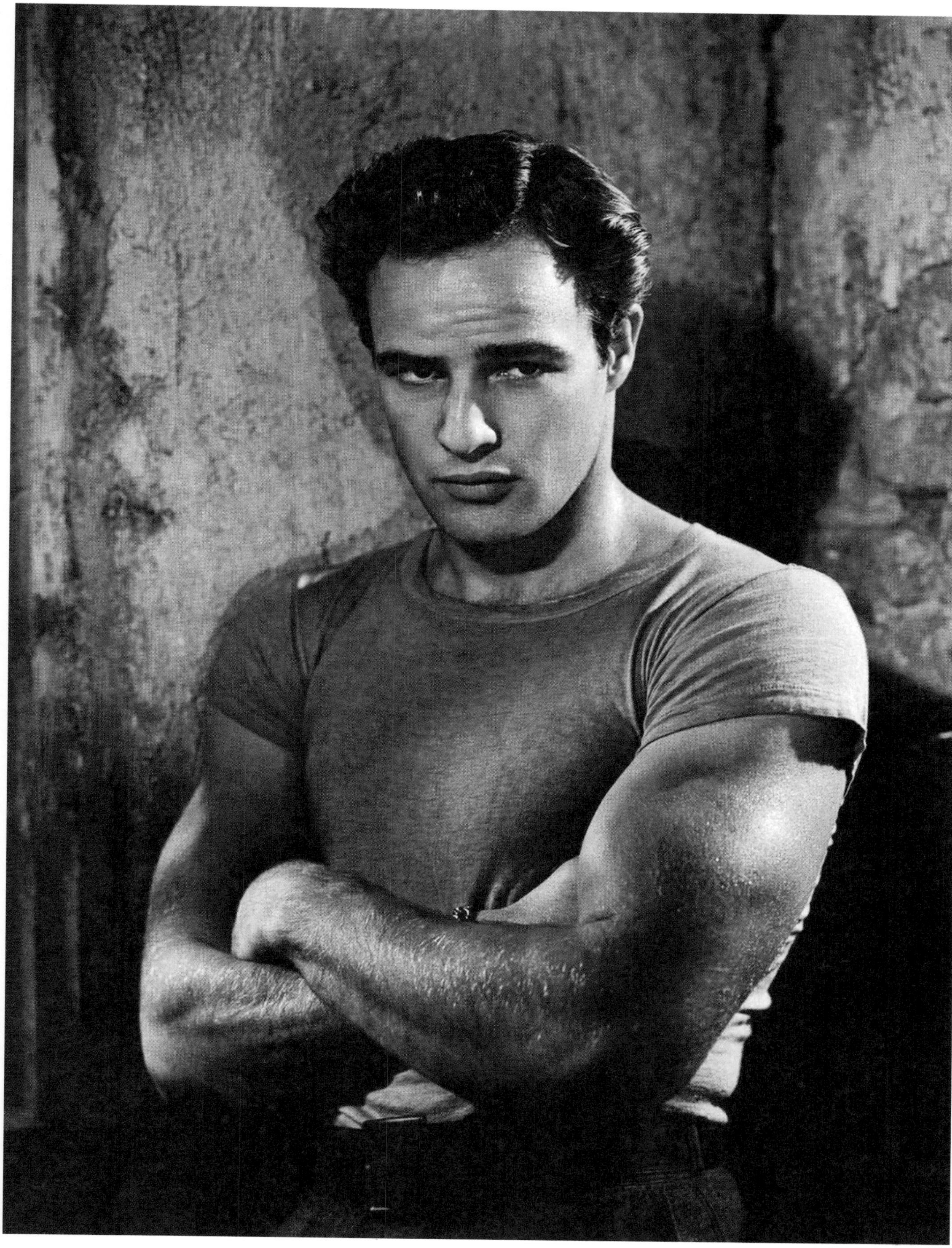

Marlon Brando in *A Streetcar Named Desire*, 1951

7 Marshall McLuhan, *Understanding Media: The Extensions of Man.*

8 Claire Wilcox, *Vivienne Westwood*, p. 12.

9 http://www.katharinehamnett.com/Campaigns/Slogan-T-Shirts//.

slogans such as 'Feminist & Proud' and 'Sisterhood is powerful' were also used as political pamphlets in the second wave of feminism, which spread gradually throughout the Western world in the early Sixties. During this period, the T-shirt itself slowly began to overshadow the slogans it carried, or as the communication theorist Marshall McLuhan put it in the mid-Sixties, "the medium is the message."[7] The T-shirt was embraced by a younger generation as the ideal medium for sharing political ideologies with the rest of the world, and so 'the T-shirt' and 'the message' became one.

The emergence of the punk movement in the Seventies lent an extra boost to this trend and the T-shirt became an ambassador for the entire body. Fashion was turned into a political statement: people sported Mohican haircuts, pierced ears, ripped clothes and platform shoes, yet the T-shirt remained the most explicit indicator of their punk identity. Reflecting this role, plus the fact that the T-shirt was cheap and easy to adapt, British fashion designer Vivienne Westwood and her then-partner Malcolm McLaren placed it at the heart of their first collections. In 1971, the duo opened their first boutique: 'Let It Rock', in the London borough of Chelsea, selling customised T-shirts. They bought simple, plain black and black-and-white striped T-shirts in bulk, which Vivienne Westwood transformed into unique creations by ripping, knotting, cutting and embroidering them or by adding feathers, zips, studs, chains and all manner of acquired objects which even included chicken bones. The T-shirts included many controversial prints and inflammatory slogans like 'Too Fast to Live, Too Young to Die' and 'Keep Warm This Winter – Make Trouble'. In 1975, Westwood and McLaren were charged with exposing the public to indecent images with their 'Cambridge Rapist' and 'Paedophilia' T-shirts. As Vivienne Westwood once said, "My job is always to confront the establishment to try and find out where freedom lies and what you can do: the most obvious way I did that was through the porn T-shirts."[8] With her provocative T-shirts, she aimed to break the taboos that her parents' generation had perpetuated.

Another designer to confront the Establishment with her T-shirts was the UK's Katharine Hamnett in the Eighties. Hamnett launched her fashion label in 1979 and introduced her first slogan T-shirts in 1983. She gained worldwide fame in 1984 for wearing one of her own T-shirts to meet Margaret Thatcher, the UK's Prime Minister at that time. It displayed the slogan '58% Don't Want Pershing' in protest against the British government's plans to base Pershing nuclear missiles at various military bases throughout the country. Hamnett's slogan T-shirts became enormously popular, not least thanks to her 'Choose Life' design appearing in a video by pop group Wham! in 1984. They also spawned an abundance of imitations. Hamnett: "To this day my slogan T-shirts are copied, worn and reiterated. From a fashion perspective it's flattering. From a political perspective, it's exactly what I set out to achieve — to sow seeds of change and help people create a voice."[9]

In the Seventies, Vivienne Westwood's T-shirts were actually only worn by a small group of people from the punk subculture, since punks tended to prefer to customise their own clothes. They refused to become a part of the official fashion scene, which was a symbol of the capitalist system. Katharine Hamnett subsequently launched and built up her own brand in the Eighties at a time when young avant-garde fashion designers were acquiring a celebrity status and when fashion was beginning to revolve around logo mania, branding and image. As a result, Hamnett was one of the first 'rebellious' designers to also become part of 'the Establishment' — something which would have been unthinkable for Westwood a decade earlier. Yet it proved to be a formula for success which is still going strong today. In 2008, Katharine Hamnett collaborated with H&M on the 'Fashion Against Aids' project, producing a range of affordable T-shirts featuring recognisable Hamnett slogans such as 'Choose Life' and 'Stop and Think'. In the spring of 2012, she created another T-shirt for H&M, this time with the slogan 'Save the Future' in support of Climate Week. The T-shirt adorned with political slogans has gone from being a controversial symbol of anti-fashion in the Seventies, to an institutionalised, accepted and 'neutralised' garment in today's fashion wardrobe.

10 Germano Celant, 'B, D and K', in: KAWS, p. 51.

FROM COMMUNICATION MEDIUM TO ART

The history of the T-shirt can be linked not only to marketing and politics, but also to the underground culture which emerged in the Seventies and included Pop Art and graffiti. Around the same time that Katharine Hamnett launched her slogan T-shirts, the artists Barbara Kruger (1945) and Jenny Holzer (1950) were also experimenting with slogans. Both of these women reflected on a range of themes including sexuality, feminism, consumerism, divisions of power and death through provocative visual statements such as 'I shop therefore I am' and 'Your body is a battleground' (Kruger), as well as 'Protect me from what I want' and 'Abuse of power comes as no surprise' (Holzer). While Kruger restricted her use of slogans to printing them on black-and-white photographs, Holzer went a step further, carving them into trees and public benches, spraying them as graffiti onto walls and bus shelters, printing them on stickers and condom packaging and even installing a billboard in Times Square. For 'Documenta VII' in 1982, the five-yearly exhibition for modern art, Holzer had her truisms printed on T-shirts and baseball caps. For this project, she worked with Stefan Eins, owner of the Fashion Moda gallery in New York's South Bronx district since 1972. Having set out to share art with a disadvantaged community, Eins saw graffiti both as a way of giving that community a voice, and as the ideal way of communicating with it. So he chose to support graffiti artists such as Keith Haring and Kenny Scharf. The collaboration with Holzer enabled him to reach members of the community even more effectively by printing graffiti art on T-shirts and baseball caps.

Barbara Kruger, *Untitled (I Shop Therefore I Am)*, 1987

Claes Oldenburg, *The Store*, installation, Green Gallery, New York, 1963

This 'artist-driven retail' concept is rooted in the Pop Art movement. Pop artist Claes Oldenburg, for example, opened 'The Store' on New York's Lower East Side in 1961 and sold products ranging from T-shirts and sculptures to food.[10] Of course, the real star of the direct commercialisation of art was Andy Warhol, who teamed up with the Bianchini Gallery in New York in 1964 to open the 'American Supermarket', where people could purchase an Andy Warhol shopping bag for just a few dollars, a box of Robert Watt eggs or other replica food items by Tom Wesselmann, Richard Artschwager or James Rosenquist. In the Eighties, the boundaries between art and merchandise became increasingly blurred, a development that peaked with the opening of Keith Haring's 'Pop Shop' in 1986. With its iconic image of 'The Radiant Baby', the store created a commercial brand which bordered on fetishism.

Jenny Holzer, *Truisms* T-shirt, 1983

The developments within the Pop Art and Minimal Art movements, in which the focus moved from the object itself to the message behind it, are noticeably similar to the way the T-shirt evolved. "Indeed the shift is away from making and towards communicating, where the privileged means of artistic thought solicits and demands greater attention and affirmation through increased dissemination, comprehensible and determinate."[11] As a result, the twenty-first century has witnessed the emergence of a new generation — a hybrid between artist and fashion designer — which uses the T-shirt as a platform for its message, yet also manages to build a reputation as a fashion designer. "It was a manifestation of energy wishing to insert its own self into the codified imagery of mass-communication, that of posters and advertising," said Germano Celant about graffiti artist and T-shirt designer KAWS.[12] In effect, their work pays homage to the endless number of new possibilities that are emerging for modern-day communication-driven culture: from graffiti and tags to logos on bags, T-shirts and caps, computers, the internet, et cetera. And according to Patricia Calefato, the T-shirt has created a link not only between fashion and art, but also between clothing and language as a social practice in our modern-day society.[13]

THE NEW GENERATION: THE RISE OF KAWS AND BAPE

Brian Donnelly (1974), better known as KAWS, grew up in the Eighties at a time when the market was awash with gadgets, toys and film merchandise from major Hollywood productions such as Star Wars and Transformers. KAWS started his artistic career by spraying graffiti on walls, trains and water towers, but upon arriving in New York in 1996, he made a transition to 'ad disruptions': adapting existing advertisements in bus shelters. With these 'interventions' as the art world calls them, his aim was not to override the advertisements, but rather to make it appear as if his illustrations were part of the original designs. He adapted posters in a Calvin Klein campaign by decorating the image of Kate Moss with a cartoon-like figure. Each figure had two X's as eyes, which became the KAWS trademark. He soon progressed from this form of graffiti to developing clothing and toys, and he received his first commission in 1999. He designed a 3D version of his, by then well-known, graffiti dolls for the Japanese fashion brand HECTIC, 1,500 of which were manufactured, followed by projects for fashion brands including Undercover (1999), Bape (2005), Marc Jacobs and Nike. "It is a way of being there, using fashion's communicative power to establish an emblem which in the end can stand alongside the other logos, thus creating art products that are recognisable because they are associated with a brand, an industrial transformation of the manual tag," says Donelly.[14] Yet he has no real ambition to gain serious recognition as an artist: "I always felt there was a hypocrisy in the fine art world, in their snobbery about products. I am never going to commit to doing just products, or just painting. I am going to do it all at the same time and see where it leads." He enjoys chafing the fashion industry by using the X's in the same way as Mercedes uses its distinct grill on its cars: "You see them in the rear-view mirror and just have a glimpse of it, and you know the style of the car going behind you."[15]

11 Germano Celant, 'B, D and K', in: KAWS, p. 46.

12 Ibid.

13 Patricia Calefato, 'Fashion as sign system', in: Jan Brand and José Teunissen (ed.), The Power of Fashion. On design and meaning, p. 150.

14 Germano Celant, 'B, D and K', in: KAWS, p. 50.

15 Germano Celant, 'B, D and K', in: KAWS, p. 49.

KAWS, *Kurfs*, 2008

The Japanese streetwear label Bape, short for A Bathing Ape, originated in Tokyo in 1993 as a T-shirt brand. Designer Tomoaki Nagao (1970), better known as Nigo, purposefully kept the brand exclusive by making and selling a limited number of each design, believing that exclusivity would guarantee the product's lasting appeal. The label's name is a reference to the spoilt teenagers of Japan, whose lives are as comfortable as a 'bathing ape in lukewarm water'. It also reflects Japanese youth culture in which comic books, games, streetwear and prêt-à-porter influences appear to converge seamlessly. Although the Bape label started out as a T-shirt brand, it soon got involved in commercial collaborations with the likes of Nintendo. Nigo took the liberty of integrating other cartoon characters such as Hello Kitty into his graphic visual language, which led to a new narrative and visual culture. When he encountered Brian Donnelly's work, he recognised a kindred spirit in KAWS despite their completely different backgrounds and cultures. So Nigo asked KAWS to design a special collection for Bape.

Nigo is aware of the crucial role the T-shirt plays in his visual language: "Just as Ralph Lauren is known for its polo shirts, the T-shirt is both a staple and a symbol of A Bathing Ape," he says. "It's expressive and uncomplicated at the same time, making it a medium best suited to our needs."[16]

Even though Bape started with a T-shirt design and KAWS did not, the two designers ultimately share the same aim. Both Nigo and Donnelly strive for a graphic presence that does not tie them to a particular product. They both express themselves in a range of disciplines and they mix their own visual languages with those of others. And in a world in which the printed T-shirt has become a staple item, this is precisely what gives these two brands unique and added value. With a KAWS or Bape T-shirt, you will feel as if you have been transported into another universe.

16 Aiko Iida and Ian Luna, *A Bathing Ape*, p. 23.

BIBLIOGRAPHY

Barthes, Roland, *Système de la mode*, Éditions du Seuil, Paris 1967.

Calefato Patricia, 'Fashion as sign systems' in Jan Brand & José Teunissen (eds.), *The Power of Fashion. On Design and Meaning*, Terra/ArtEZ Press, Arnhem 2006, pp. 126–152.

Calefato, Patricia, 'Language and fashion. From the name of God to the power of the brand' in Jan Brand & José Teunissen (eds.), *Fashion and Imagination*, d'jonge Hond/ArtEZ Press, Arnhem 2009, pp. 126–138.

Celant, Germano, 'B, D and K' in *KAWS*, Rizzoli, New York 2010 pp. 46–56.

Hollander, Anne, *Sex and Suits*, Knopf, New York 1994.

Iida, Aiko and Luna, Ian, *A Bathing Ape*, Rizzoli, New York 2008.

Kuyper, Eric de, *De verbeelding van het mannelijk lichaam*, Sun, Nijmegen 1993.

McCormick, Carlo, 'KAWS' in *Juxtapoz*, Summer 2004, 33.

Wilcox, Claire, *Vivienne Westwood*, London's Victoria & Albert Museum 2004.

Left: Bape x Spongebob, T-shirt, 2008
Above: Bape matches, promoting the new store in in Harajuku, January 2008

Comme des Garçons SHIRT advertisement, by Megan Kelso, A/W 2000–2001

Since the re-emergence of the DIY hype (do-it-your-self) in which clothing is customised to give it a personal twist, the T-shirt has become a DIY icon and an influential medium. It has been deconstructed in terms of its shape and its meaning.

The idea of deconstructing the classic T-shirt to create a vehicle of expression came from British designer Vivienne Westwood (1941) and her partner Malcolm McLaren (1946–2010) in the 1970s. Their anarchistic, punk-themed T-shirts were inspired by the prints and techniques used by Situationists, in essence revolving around creating chaos (general-ly being destructive) and provoking an artistic and political revolution (destroying things in order to put something else in their place).

Vivienne Westwood met British artist and man-ager of punk band the Sex Pistols Malcolm McLaren in 1965. Known as an eccentric fashion designer, Westwood was attracted to McLaren's alternative views and subversive lifestyle. In 1971, the two joined forces, opening a London clothes shop 'Let it Rock at Paradise Garage' which was subsequently renamed several times. It became 'Too Fast to Live Too Young to Die' in 1973, 'SEX' in 1974, 'Seditionaries' in 1976, and then 'World Ends', the name the store still holds to this day.

In the course of the Seventies, a subculture grew around the shop which eventually evolved into the Punk and New Wave movements. The store sold Westwood's provocative designs that poked fun at the aristocratic style of the British Royal Family. McLaren added bondage and S&M elements to the designs, such as gashes, safety pins and bicycle chains. Their rebellious 'bricolage' T-shirts really caught on when Westwood took charge of styling the Sex Pistols themselves. The ripped, dirty T-shirts displaying de-fiant graphic prints, offensive slogans and decorated with safety pins, served as wearable statements against authority, consumerism and the humble citizen. McLaren in particular yearned to bring about a social revolution by creating disruptive situations surrounding the band's performances. As he hoped, the scandalous T-shirts were purchased by countless fans who saw them as a form of rebellion against the Establishment: shirts screen-printed with the words 'God save the queen – She ain't no human being', a safety pin piercing Queen Elizabeth's lips or letters cut from newspaper headlines over her eyes and mouth with the Union Jack in tatters behind it. But it was the 'Destroy' T-shirt — a straitjacket printed with an inverted crucifix, a swastika and a small image of Her Majesty — that caused the most controversy. The shirts were primarily intended as an attack on the government, the Church and the fascist values that were prevalent at the time, rather than the monarchy itself.

McLaren's and Westwood's T-shirts are iconic and have laid the foundations for DIY T-shirts by other designers ever since. Furthermore, deliberate rips in clothes such as jeans, bondage details, safety pins and the stonewashed look, all contain a hint of rebel-lion, defiance and rock & roll. But what the punk style created by McLaren and Westwood really embodied was the urge to change the rules by deconstructing accepted patterns and designs. Thanks to both the symbolism of, and the printed art in, their fashion, they succeeded in creating an entire subculture of their own, one which later evolved into an artistic movement; something no other fashion designer has managed to do since.

www.viviennewestwood.co.uk

Vivienne Westwood's London clothes shop 'SEX' in 1977

Vivienne Westwood and friends in her London shop 'SEX', 1977

Katharine Hamnett meets Margaret Thatcher dressed in one of her own T-shirts, 1984

A designer of children's clothing and fashion for so-cially conscious men and women, Katharine Hamnett (1948) achieved global fame in the 1980s with her pro-test T-shirts. Immediately after graduating in fashion from St. Martins School of Arts & Design in London in 1969, she and her college friend, Anne Buck, founded the sports label 'TUTTABANKEN', which soon built up an international reputation in the women's fashion in-dustry. In 1979, Katharine Hamnett went independent using her own name, and in 1981, she started design-ing menswear.

Tired of fame, she set out in search of the kind of fulfilment that the fashion industry had yet failed to bring her. Influenced by Buddhism, she introduced her first protest shirt in 1983: an oversized white T-shirt with 'CHOOSE LIFE' printed in large black capital letters on the front. It held immense and immediate appeal for key figures in the music industry, the street scene and the art world including Wham! and Boy George, who were among the first to wear her shirts. It was no coincidence that Hamnett turned to the T-shirt again in the Eighties as a vehicle for commu-nicating the need for a social uprising. At that time, the world was gripped by the threat of nuclear war, environmental pollution, destruction of the rainforests and the lack of democracy in the politics of Margaret Thatcher and Ronald Reagan, who were not prepared to listen to the voice of the people. In response, Hamnett wore a large white shirt reading '58% don't want Pershing' to a meeting with Prime Minister Margaret Thatcher. The iconic photo became repre-sentative of Hamnett's subsequent career in fashion, and her mission to better the world continued beyond simply spreading socio-political messages.

In addition to her fashion collections, Hamnett continues to produce new protest shirts made from organic cotton, which she hopes will be copied. Thanks to Hamnett, slogan shirts have become an integral part of modern-day popular culture whilst the mass media has given them a wide and very public audience, making them a popular way for artists and people in the public eye to create an image for themselves. There are countless examples of this: the 'Vote or Die!' shirt (2004) that has been worn by celebrities such as Paris Hilton, or the 'Occupy [W]all Street[s]' shirt Jay Z wore during his live shows (2011). Both of these shirts were intended to speak to young Ameri-cans through popular culture and stir them into taking political action. Plenty of other fashion designers put the power of words into good use too. Take the House of Holland for example that mocks the fashion scene with phrases like 'Cause me pain Hedi Slimane' and 'Flick yer bean for Agyness Deyn' (2007). Meanwhile, Nike's 'Just Do It' slogan dating back to 1988 and 'Be Stupid' by Diesel from 2010 are examples of slogans which have transcended the brands, turning the T-shirt into a form of free advertising.

www.katharinehamnett.com

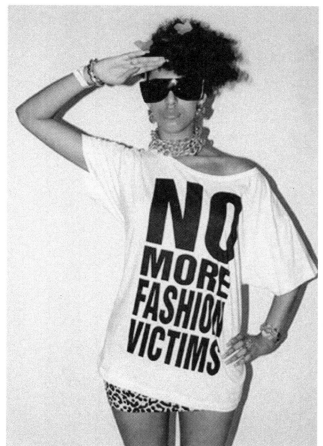

Katharine Hamnett, *Save the Future*

The Japanese streetwear label Bape, short for 'A Bathing Ape', was founded in 1993 by Tomoaki Nagao (1970), better known as Nigo. The label's name refers to members of Japan's spoilt younger generation, whose indulgent lifestyles he likened to a "bathing ape in lukewarm water".

Bape started out as a highly exclusive label. In its first two years, Nigo produced between thirty and fifty T-shirts per week, giving half of them to friends and selling the rest. Nigo ran his label from a small shop in the Harajuku district of Tokyo, in the days before it became annexed by the young and trendy. Word soon spread about Bape, but despite long queues forming in front of the door, Nigo resisted the temptation to increase production. His reasoning was that limiting the availability would lead to a further surge in demand and ensure his Bape T-shirts retained their aura of exclusivity.

Since 1997, Nigo has worked with various commercial partners. The first collaboration saw him releasing an album with the British hip-hop label Mo'Wax. He also launched a clothing label called Billionaire Boys Club with rapper Pharrell Wiliams, which was followed by projects with the likes of Marvel, Nintendo, DC Comics, MAC make-up, Pepsi, Carhartt and Casio. Nigo also combined the Bape graphics with well-known cartoon characters such as Hello Kitty, SpongeBob SquarePants, and customised images by graffiti artist KAWS.

In the meantime, it has become easier to get hold of Bape clothing as Nigo has opened Bape flagship stores right around the world, and a webshop further extended his retail activities in 2005.

It is their strong, graphic style that ensures that Bape products are so recognisable. The label makes heavy use of a number of logos, the first of which is Bape, based on the ape called Cornelius in the film *Planet of the Apes* (1968). Cornelius also features in the Bape camouflage print. The second logo is Baby Milo, a simple cartoon drawing of a baby monkey, representing Cornelius's son. And for the Bape sneakers, Nigo developed the Bapesta, a logo reminiscent of the Nike 'swoosh'. Other recurring graphics include the slogan 'Ape shall never kill ape', the 'ape generals' and fast-food prints.

www.bape.com

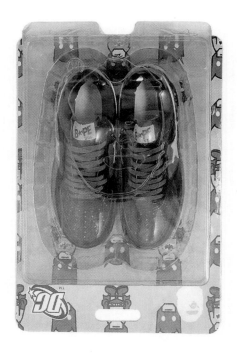

Above: Nigo in Bape camouflage print, 2006
Below: DC x Bape Sta sneakers, A/W 2007–2008

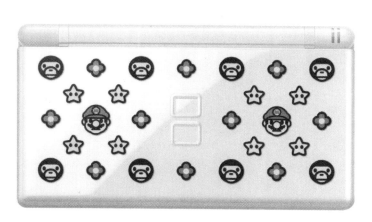

Above: Bape sweater, S/S 1995
Below: A Bathing Ape for Nintendo DS Lite, 2008; Baby Milo x KAWS, 2005

Having studied at the School of Visual Arts in New York, Brian Donnelly (1974), better known as KAWS, started his career in the mid-Nineties as a freelance animator at Disney, where he worked on TV series including *101 Dalmatians*, *Daria* and *Doug*. In his free time, KAWS was a prolific graffiti artist who decorated billboards and advertising posters in bus shelters and phone boxes. Initially, he surreptitiously broke the glass display cases open, until a friend gave him a skeleton key that could open any case, anywhere in the world. In his 'ad disruptions', as KAWS called them, he added his own illustrations to existing posters, with advertisements relating to fashion and lifestyle being his favourite to 'adapt'. KAWS's artistic style was one of clean lines with no brushstrokes, so that his additions would appear to be part of the original advertisements. Within a few short months, posters featuring KAWS's work were being stolen from bus shelters and sold for considerable sums of money on the black market.

The KAWS style is universally recognisable. The figures in his drawings are often variations on well-known cartoon characters such as SpongeBob SquarePants, The Smurfs, The Simpsons and Mickey Mouse. KAWS has even created his own character called Chum, a version of the Michelin Man but with his head resembling a skull and crossbones, and crosses where his eyes should be. Incidentally, the latter is a distinguishing feature of all the characters in KAWS's drawings.

KAWS's graffiti gradually moved from the streets to canvas, and in the late Nineties he started producing limited-edition vinyl dolls. Based on the cartoon figures in his graffiti works and paintings, they proved particularly popular in Japan. Around the same time, he joined forces with Medicom Toy to open the OriginalFake store in the Aoyama district of Tokyo, selling not only his toys but clothing too. KAWS also started collaborating with fashion labels such as Marc Jacobs, Bape, Comme des Garçons, Nike and Vans, and the Kiehls cosmetics brand.

In his work, KAWS manages to cleverly combine art and commercialism, making no distinction between the two — just as one of his major sources of inspiration, Keith Haring.

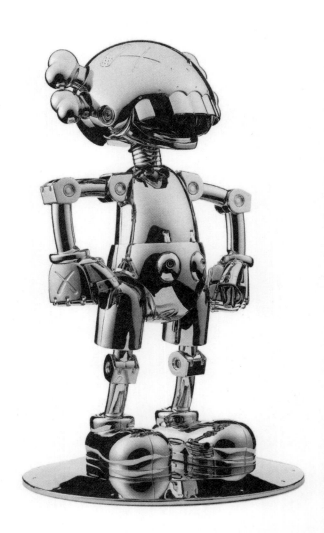

Above: KAWS T-shirt
Right: KAWS toy
Right page: KAWS 'ad disruption'

Even those who don't recognise his name might well recognise his work, especially if they live in The Netherlands. Illustrations by Pieter Janssen (1976), better known as Piet Parra, are widespread in the Dutch Randstad area, from T-shirts by his fashion label Rockwell to posters and flyers advertising a number of Amsterdam clubs and performances by Dutch rappers such as Extince, Kubus and Opgezwolle.

Piet Parra grew up in Limburg, living with his father, artist Willem Janssen. Parra's great passion was skateboarding — he made it to semi-professional level and Vans even sponsored his shoes. He became Dutch champion in 1996, but after discovering he was not quite good enough to compete at international level, he needed to re-think his future. Having been rejected by art college, Piet Parra embarked on a teacher training course after secondary school. Despite hating every minute of it, he stuck it out until the third year. A work experience placement at an advertising/internet agency in Amsterdam opened his eyes; he decided to quit his course and stay on at the company instead. Parra ended up working there for three years on all manner of advertising campaigns, websites, typography and illustrations. In his spare time, he created flyers for parties. The flyers evolved into posters and the posters into album covers and, slowly but surely, Piet Parra designs became increasingly prevalent on the Amsterdam street scene.

In 2006, Piet Parra joined forces with his good friend Alexander Rommens to launch clothing label Rockwell. Having started out with a series of T-shirts featuring Parra designs, the label soon expanded to include jumpers and caps, and nowadays the Rockwell range includes towels, duvet covers, slippers and even shower curtains. Piet Parra began attracting a growing number of commercial projects: IBM, Heineken, Footlocker and Hi, and streetwear and sportswear brands such as Vans, Nike, Converse and Stüssy, have all used Piet Parra's illustrations.

In 2009, Piet Parra designed a mini-collection for Nike, including a range of T-shirts, a bomber jacket and a pair of Nike Air Max shoes, which he called 'Lovely underachieving loners'. "Nike is always about winning, isn't it? That's why I made this jacket, as a tribute to all the losers," said Parra about the collection. That sense of humour is characteristic of his style, and he enjoys rooting for the underdog. In addition to being inspired by Kamagurka and Monty Python, he was also influenced by his father, who — like Parra himself — enjoyed painting animals and voluptuous women. In Parra's works, the women often have beaks, which he has said have a similar effect as masks and take the edge off the potential offensiveness of the rest of the image. His reasoning is that it's harder to get angry about the drawings when the women look like that. Another recognisable feature of Piet Parra's work is the hand-drawn lettering. His illustrations are created by hand too, using a regular pen from no-nonsense Dutch retailer HEMA. He then takes a photo with his iPhone, uploads it onto his computer and fine-tunes his drawings using Illustrator software, either in characteristic Parra colours such as electric blue, deep red and shocking pink, or in simple black and white.

Despite the fact that his work has been included in the San Francisco MOMA collection and that his drawings have been displayed in galleries from Tokyo and Los Angeles to Paris and London, Piet Parra still questions whether he can call himself a real artist. He says he accepts large-scale commercial projects, such as for a dogfood manufacturer in the UK, because they pay the bills, and that's what enables him to work on his own drawings and sculptures in his free time.

Since 2007 Piet Parra has been making music too, in a group called Le Le formed together with Pepijn Lanen from Dutch band De Jeugd Van Tegenwoordig and DJ/producer Rimer London.

www.byparra.com

Left: Piet Parra limited edition artist series in porcelain,
produced in collaboration with Case Studyo, 2012
Above and right: Piet Parra for Vans,
sneakers, T-shirt, advertisement, 2009

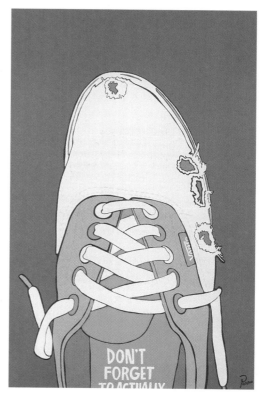

Top: Keith Haring in his *Pop Shop*
Below left and right: Nicholas Kirkwood shoes with a Keith Haring print
displayed at the Arnhem Mode Biënnale, 2011

"You use whatever comes along," said Keith Haring in an in-depth interview with *Rolling Stone Magazine* in 1989, a year before he died of AIDS aged thirty-one. The young New York-based street and pop art artist lived for his art — no limits and no compromises.

As a young homosexual from Pennsylvania, he could not bear the thought of the predictable, conservative family lifestyle that lay ahead of him there, so he moved to the hedonistic city of New York when he was nineteen. He was always drawing and began sketching simple, abstract graffiti figures in white chalk on the walls of metro stations and playgrounds; a style that helped to shape his reputation. This was his way of reaching ordinary people with his art — a typical characteristic of the pop art of the 1980s. He did not believe in the power the elite world of galleries and curators had, preferring instead the mantra of that time: 'Do it yourself'.

Haring infiltrated the wild art and club scene of New York, he became friends with the likes of Andy Warhol, Roy Lichtenstein, Jean-Michel Basquiat, Madonna and Yoko Ono. Nightclubs, drugs, sex and popular culture clearly influenced his work, but for him, it was not about rebellion and escapism: it was a way of releasing his creative spirit.

Haring: "Psychedelic shapes would come like automatic writing, out of my unconscious." He drew people, animals and UFOs with thick contours, creating a unique and symbolic visual language of his own, one that was derived from semiotics. He was fond of including sociopolitical messages in his work: he would confront people with topics such as AIDS, apartheid, hard drugs, homosexuality, love, war, birth and death. Graffiti was his poetry, the sketched figures his words.

In 1982 he held his first solo exhibition in the renowned Tony Shafrazi Gallery in New York's SoHo district. Graffiti art was very hot in the art world at that time, but Haring did not allow himself to be exploited. He opened his own store, *Pop Shop* (1986–2005), where he sold all manner of clothing, toys, posters and other items featuring his artistic designs. The interior was decorated from floor to ceiling with Haring's distinct black and white sketches, even the fixtures and fittings. It was almost like a nightclub.

His mission was twofold: firstly, to make a bold statement to the art world that art should be accessible for everyone, and secondly, to use his fame for the benefit of society as a whole. After discovering he was HIV-positive, he set up the Keith Haring Foundation (1989) in order to donate profits from royalties and merchandise to AIDS research and children's projects. Since his death, Haring has not just been admired and imitated, but also criticised for his commercialism, high productivity and childlike simplicity.

To this day, Haring's infectious iconography continues to appeal to fashion designers, artists and purveyors of popular culture, including Comme des Garçons, Levi's, Adidas and most recently, shoe designer Nicolas Kirkwood.

www.haring.com

Danish fashion label Mads Nørgaard initially started out as a store. In 1986, Mads Mathias Nørgaard (1961) opened a shop on Strøget in the centre of Copenhagen, specialising in men's fashion and including a few of Nørgaard's own designs. After subsequently opening a second store and a café, Nørgaard launched his first complete menswear line in 1995, and a women's line followed shortly afterwards, in 1996. His sober, restrained designs with the odd luxurious detail here and there were well received, and before long, Mads Nørgaard clothing was available all over the world. Nørgaard's design philosophy is based on the idea that fashion should support and free people rather than overrule or control them. It's for that reason — and also because Nørgaard believes that the Western world is moving too fast at times — that his collections are built up around a number of fashionable basics. In addition, the Mads Nørgaard collections always include a number of graphic T-shirts, often featuring slogans of a slightly political nature. His stores have a very graphic look about them too, with the characteristically bold, black lettering on their walls and windows conveying messages that typify the Nørgaard philosophy, such as: "What you wear should support you in your ways and beliefs."

Alongside designing for his Mads Nørgaard label, Nørgaard himself is regularly involved in notable projects. In March 2007, he designed a series of costumes for the American Mixture ballet, for example, and in 2008 he was invited to create a 'skin' for iGoogle, Google's personalised homepage. Other contributors have included Phillip Starck, Coldplay, Ivana Helsinki, Oscar de la Renta, Dolce & Gabbana and Diane von Furstenberg. Also in 2008, Nørgaard designed the album sleeve for Sound of Copenhagen, a mix album specially produced by DJs Kjeld Tolstrup and Le Gammeltof to mark the Copenhagen Fashion Week. In September 2009, Mads Nørgaard joined forces with artist Garder Eide Eimarsson to create a T-shirt in support of the exhibition 'The World Is Yours' in Copenhagen's Louisiana Museum of Modern Art. In another project, in 2010, Nørgaard collaborated with nine other renowned Danish designers to revamp the packaging of the country's popular Ga-Jol throat lozenges. And his collaboration with artist duo Elmgreen & Dragset was truly unique: in the summer of 2012, the artists unveiled Han, their male version of the Little Mermaid statue that can be found on Copenhagen's Langelinie, and Nørgaard had the honour of designing a T-shirt for the project.

http://madsnorgaard.dk

Left: Mads Nørgaard T-shirt, S/S 2013
Above: Mads Nørgaard for GaJol throat lozenges, 2010
Right: Mads Nørgaard, poster, 2010

WHAT YOU WEAR SHOULD SUPPORT YOU IN YOUR WAYS AND BELIEFS

MARC & THE MONOGRAM

— NANDA VAN DEN BERG

American designer Marc Jacobs is regarded as one of the most influential fashion designers of his generation. He picks up 'fashion signals' and transmits them to the rest of the industry like an antenna, a talent which was discovered soon after he graduated from the Parsons School of Design with flying colours in 1985. This was brought to the fore in the autumn of 1992 while Jacobs was working for Perry Ellis and styled the models in his 'grunge collection' to look as if they were wearing second-hand clothes. In his own words: "I wanted them to look the way they do when they walk down the street, which is not dolled up [...] That's the way beautiful girls look today: they look a little bit unconcerned about fashion."[1] He went on to develop a successful clothing style under his own brand name, one characterised by its slightly odd proportions — oversized buttons, rounded lapels, three-quarter-length sleeves, shoulders that are slightly too narrow — and an almost childlike sense of delight. "Awkwardness gives me great comfort," says Jacobs about the language of his designs[2], but perhaps his most controversial work has been for Louis Vuitton, a prestigious brand dating back some one hundred fifty years. He was recruited in 1997 to design menswear and womenswear collections to help introduce its classic, luxury brand of leather goods as a fashion brand. While his collections for Louis Vuitton have always caused a stir, they have never been easy to get hold of since they have always been earmarked for reinforcing the fashion house's image, mainly at shows, for publicity purposes. Louis Vuitton's core business is still its bags, suitcases and other leather goods, all adorned with the famous monogram that has become one of the most iconic fashion graphics of our time.[3] The letters LV, the founder's initials, are displayed prominently, like ornaments in the architecture of its stores designed especially to support the brand, and have featured as a motif in the company's art since the early Nineties. Whilst the latter should be regarded as a classical expression of this illustrious brand, the contemporary incarnation of the LV monogram has, in contrast, been put in the hands of Marc Jacobs, a designer whose work tends to lack any kind of formal logic: "I often feel uncomfortable," Jacobs says.

"I have this feeling like this is only going to be good as long as it's good. Am I always full of ideas? No. Those things don't happen every six months. It's not

1 Dan Shaw, 'To Make His Own Marc', in: *The New York Times*, 28 February 1993.

2 Amy Larocca, 'Marc Jacobs' Paradoxical Triumph', in: *New York Magazine*, 21 August 2005.

3 For a detailed overview of these, see *Louis Vuitton, Art, Fashion and Architecture*, New York 2009.

even like, 'You have to change the shape of handbags and the luxury market.' It's like, 'This has to change the shape of history.' And I don't know how to calculate that. I really don't."[4] What then, one might ask, could this informal and completely intuitive approach to such a historically charged monogram tell us about the direction fashion is taking?

4 In Larocca, op. cit. (note 2).

5 Murray Healy, 'Marc on Sprouse', in: *Pop*, nr. 13, p. 282.

6 Ibid.

7 Patricia Morrisroe, 'Stephen Sprouse – The Punk Glamour God', in: *New York Magazine*, 5 April 2004.

8 Roger Padilha in Roger & Mauricio Padilha, *Stephen Sprouse*, New York 2009.

THE ICONOCLAST

That Marc Jacobs can indeed influence the direction of fashion was demonstrated in 2001 by his 'Speedy Bag', which was covered in graffiti by Stephen Sprouse. This took the discussion about prestige brands — and the Louis Vuitton brand in particular — to the next level, something very few other luxury products had achieved. It freed the brand from its chains of exclusivity and propelled it into the world of art and popular culture.

Since the 'Speedy Bag', Louis Vuitton has become better known by a wider public, one that up until that time was not even aware of luxury brands.[5] According to Jacobs, the idea of emblazoning the classic LV pattern with Sprouse's graffiti originated from "this Louis Vuitton trunk that Serge had had painted over black, for some reason," which he happened to discover in the corner of singer and actress Charlotte Gainsbourg's apartment.[6] While it is not clear when exactly Serge Gainsbourg had committed the deed, the energy involved in radically repainting something like this, brings the year 1968 to mind — the year that Serge Gainsbourg achieved major international fame thanks to his duet *Je t'aime moi non plus* with Charlotte's mother, Jane Birkin.

And it was in the Sixties that the younger generation emerged as a 'third class' and rebelled against society's established order. This happened with words and with deeds, but the teenagers also seemed to want to underline their hard-won social status in an explicitly visual and graphic manner. Sixties' fashion is typified by boxy proportions, heavy-handed black eyeliner and geometric hairstyles; the Pop Art movement by thick contours and kinetic art by vibrating lines. This clearly youthful and energetic style continued into subsequent decades, with successive new generations wanting to feel 'forever young'. Then when Malcolm McLaren and Vivienne Westwood started printing voyeuristic punk slogans on garments in 1975, and selling them through their boutique called 'Sex', clothing came to equal language. In the years that followed, graffiti became commonplace in towns and cities: walls, underground stations and tunnels were daubed with tags, slogans and doodles. Graffiti merged with art in the work of Jean Michel Basquiat and Keith Haring, and their contemporary Stephen Sprouse, who had always scribbled his friends' telephone numbers all over his hands and arms, fused graffiti with fashion. As the story goes, Stephen Sprouse was walking through the East Village one day in 1983, "and suddenly he went home and began sketching graffiti-covered motorcycle jackets and sequined miniskirts."[7] According to his biographers, Sprouse's designs were "one of the first definitive visual signatures of Eighties fashion."[8]

Yet graffiti is far from reticent — it is very hard to ignore. Norman Mailer wrote that "graffiti screams your ego across the city," and by inviting Stephen Sprouse to scrawl the words 'Louis Vuitton' over the LV monogram in 2001, Marc Jacobs had in fact challenged the Establishment. The reputation of this

Marc Jacobs carrying a Louis Vuitton bag designed by Stephen Sprouse, photographed by Terry Richardson, 2010

Keith Me, photographed by David Sims, styling by Carine Roitfeld, *Vogue Paris* November 2009

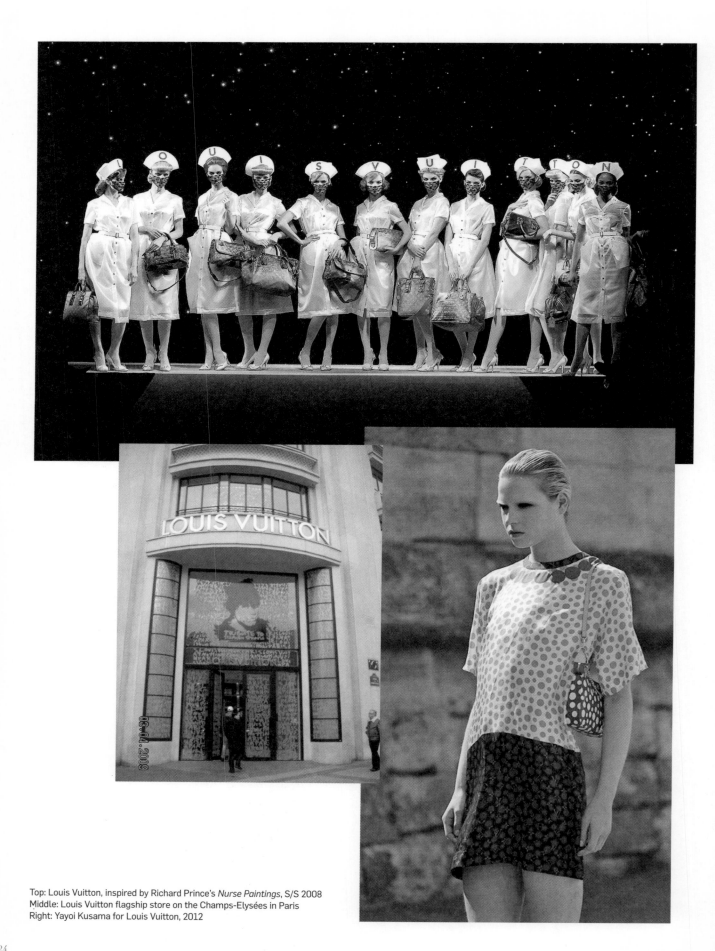

Top: Louis Vuitton, inspired by Richard Prince's *Nurse Paintings*, S/S 2008
Middle: Louis Vuitton flagship store on the Champs-Elysées in Paris
Right: Yayoi Kusama for Louis Vuitton, 2012

luxury brand has always been inextricably linked with the classic grace of its monogram; it dates from the nineteenth century when 'personalised luxury' was invented by a number of unique creatives such as Worth, Boucheron, Guerlain and Vuitton who, for the first time in history, hit on the idea of raising the value of their prestigious products by adding their names to them. The LV monogram went on to become an exclusive sign of distinction for travel-related products, carrying associations of quality, craftsmanship and above all, a sense of the everlasting; a reputation that lasted for more than a century until Marc Jacobs threw 'pop culture luxury'[9] into the mix. Marc Jacobs was in charge of the monogram.

His designs for Louis Vuitton establish a new kind of luxury. "The way I define luxury isn't by fabric or fibre or the amount of gold bits hanging from it," says Jacobs, "That's an old definition. For me, luxury is about pleasing yourself, not dressing for other people."[10] With Marc Jacobs at the helm, Louis Vuitton worked with various leading artists personally admired by Jacobs, such as Takashi Murakami (2003), Richard Prince (2008) and Yayoi Kusama (2012), automatically making the monogram a topic of great discussion in fashionable and artistic circles. While the topic has fallen in and out of fashion, the energy and the originality of the abovementioned collaborations have Marc Jacobs's own sense of personal luxury to thank. Now that he has united the worlds of art, luxury and personal enjoyment with the world of fashion, and in view of the fact that fashion continually demands change, one question remains: what will Marc subject the monogram to next?

THE NARCISSIST

No one really knows where fashion will take us, of course, but there is a clear link between fashion and the way we live: we are inclined to think it can foretell the future. In 1924, the spiritual thinker and teacher Gerald Heard (1889–1971)[11] wrote in *Narcissus. An Anatomy of Clothes*[12]: "On the physical plane, Radium we have been told is a survival from an earlier form of matter. Clothes it can be shown are, on the psychological, as singular a continuance. In them and them alone there is at the present day what once has been but now is transcended in all the other habits of man, an organic, impersonal development, not analogous but homologous with his physical evolution."[13] Heard further claimed "that evolution is going on no longer in but around man, and the faster because working in a less resistant medium. Man becomes like a wireless valve, a transmitter which in the process immensely amplifies the current he receives," and concluded that man is "not completed [...] He shall finish the story as he likes."[14]

When viewed from a contemporary perspective, that last statement suddenly has a prophetic ring to it. In an essay about the future of beauty, sociologist Philippe Liotard predicts the twenty-first century will be one of 'do-it-yourself appearances' characterised by rebellious beauty ideals, androgyny, a multitude of hybrid styles and manipulation of the body "to sculpt beauty according to each person's desire." The philosopher Lipovetsky writes that he expects to see unbridled consumerism, while "an unprecedented fixation on personal happiness, and extreme individualism [...] has invented a new form of narcissism [...] Never before has the body been such a focus of attention, protection and

9 Jill Gasparina, 'Art Essay. 33 Colors', op. cit. (note 1), pp. 41–48.

10 Dana Thomas, *Deluxe. How luxury lost its luster*, New York 2007, p. 17.

11 According to Wikipedia: "historian, science writer, educator and philosopher".

12 Gerald Heard, *Narcissus. An Anatomy of Clothes*, London 1924.

13 Ibid., p. 15.

14 Ibid.

15 Philippe Liotard, 'Do-it-yourself aesthetics', pp. 42, 43, 45, and Gilles Lipovetsky 'Ego building', in: 'Future and Projections', part 5 of Elizabeth Azoulay (eds.), *100 000 years of beauty*, Paris 2009; pp. 48–50.

prevention." Our behaviour is driven by "individual maximisation of happiness and narcissistic physical ideals."[15]

Similarly, Marc Jacobs has undergone a striking physical transformation in recent years, attracting considerable attention from the media. His metamorphosis has been from a "chubby Jewish guy with long hair and glasses" into someone with short hair and contact lenses "who looks like a cartoon superhero: muscular, bronzed, shining with diamonds."[16] When Marc Jacobs became ill with ulcerative colitis, the only way to avoid a removal operation was to alter his diet and lifestyle, but the gym turned into his temple along the way: "I love going to the gym, I love exercising — it helps me sleep better. I feel much more secure with my body and in some ways I can relate more to the joys a woman gets in terms of taking care of herself [...] Now I get up early in the morning and I really enjoy getting dressed and putting lotions on my skin and getting manicures — all those things. It's a joy, it is really nice. I like beautiful environments. I like to eat well. I think I gained an appreciation for things that I had taken for granted. I just thought that I had to be in the office and that I had to work all the time but now I enjoy so much more than just working. It is the pure result of taking care of myself."[17] Jacobs is now keen to show off the results of all that exercise. He recently posed naked, reclining on shiny foil, with a large, strategically placed perfume bottle in an advertisement for his first male fragrance 'Bang'. "Narcissus," writes Lipovetsky, "Once simply *Homo aestheticus*, is now *Homo consumericus* as well."

However, Lipovetsky concludes: "While retaining hedonistic values, Narcissus is moving farther and farther away from the pleasures of carpe diem, embracing a lifestyle that imposes the monitoring of the self, the transformation of physical appearance and an obsession with hygiene. This is not delight and pleasure in the self, but simply narcissistic anxiety coupled with an endless search for information, reassurance and self-reflexivity."[18] Marc Jacobs agrees, as he demonstrated in his statement: "My opinion about myself is so based on what other people think of me. So when people said nice things about the way I looked, it helped me to feel like I wanted to do more of it."[19]

How can such a 'narcissistic anxiety' be translated into a new vision for the LV monogram? Jacobs chose to parade his models down the catwalk in the Louis Vuitton menswear show in 2010 with scarves and bags adorned with tigers and dragons. The iconography conjured up images of an exotic tattoo parlour at the end of a long sea voyage, echoing the travel theme that has been so fundamental to the rich history of this luxury luggage brand. Particularly striking was the fact that the LV monogram had been 'tattooed' around the models' necks.

The show was organised under the artistic supervision of tattoo artist Scott Campbell, of whom Marc Jacobs is a regular patron; Jacobs was just sixteen when he had his first piercing done at Body Manipulations in San Francisco and his first tattoo on Sunset Boulevard.[20] By 2012, that number had grown to 33, according to Vogue. This obsession with uniquely decorating one's own body fits in with a blurring of the boundaries between genders and cultures, the street and the catwalk. "Soft contours, ambiguous practices, shifting ideologies and nomadic lifestyles are very much a sign of the times, and likewise bring a baroque sensibility up to date," writes sociologist Michel Maffesoli.[21] It is a sensibility that is ideally suited to being expressed through

16 Ariel Levy, 'Enchanted. The transformation of Marc Jacobs', in: *The New Yorker*, 1 September 2008.

17 Marc Jacobs, *The Talks*, online magazine, 18 January 2012.

18 Lipovetsky, op. cit. (note 15).

19 Jonathan Van Meter, 'A man for all seasons', in: *US Vogue*, January 2012, p. 128.

20 Idem, p. 127.

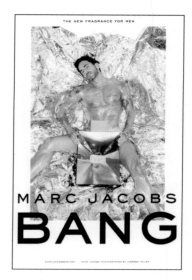

Advertisement for Marc Jacobs perfume *Bang*, photographed by Juergen Teller, 2010

personal, graphic designs on the surface — such as the skin, the tongue, the ears — of the modern-day person.

Marc Jacobs has gone on to apply his obsession with his own skin to the leather hides used by Louis Vuitton as the very essence of the luxury brand. He asked Scott Campbell to tattoo the bags with not only tigers and dragons, but also the exclusive monogram in what looks like a fine outline of the L and the V, almost stamped into the expensive leather. By literally inserting the letters of the luxury brand right into the very material it was made of, Jacobs took the monogram yet another step further than painting over it with graffiti as he did a decade earlier.

It is hard to predict what Marc Jacobs will do with the monogram next, but in his hands, and based on what we have seen over the past fifteen years, the principally static LV monogram will come even closer to becoming a dynamic projection of the future. If the artists' visions in *Future and Projections*[22] are anything to go by, the body — or actually the absence of it due to robotic techniques and technological applications — will play an ever greater role in the future; a greater role, but in a different context to clothing and luxury goods as we know them today. Perhaps the core business of bags and suitcases on which Louis Vuitton's long-standing reputation has been built will ultimately have to surrender to another, independent use of the LV monogram, one that is even more in line with the way it has been evolving under Marc Jacobs for some time. In this way, even if luxury leather goods should ever become obsolete, there will still be an emblem that can be etched into the skin, inlaid with jewels, applied using a laser or maybe even absorbed by the bloodstream; one that will ensure Louis Vuitton's name lives on into the next age of fashion.

21 Michel Maffesoli in op. cit. (note 15).

22 Op. cit. (note 15).

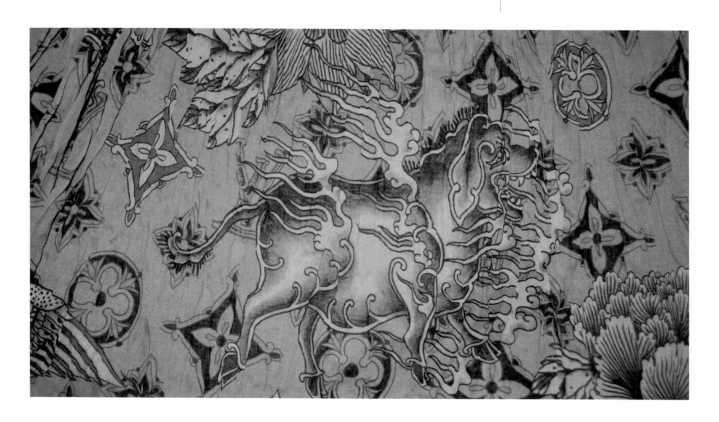

FASHION & GRAPHIC DESIGN: IDIOSYNCRATIC VISUAL LANGUAGE AS A TOTAL CONCEPT

— ELS DE BAAN

Fashion pioneer Sonia Delaunay, subsequent innovator Walter Van Beirendonck and today's contemporaries Bernhard Willhelm, Bas Kosters and Henrik Vibskov are certainly similar in some aspects of their work, but by no means all. With her quest for a new graphic-based visual language, Russian-French designer Delaunay (1885–1979) was way ahead of her time. Likewise, the work of each of these modern-day designers is diffused with an unmistakable, idiosyncratic style — one that is based around a total concept and just like Delaunay, a 'total look', which they use to create their own universes and with which they are not afraid to experiment. Their designs are as unique as their handwriting; something that can only be achieved with a distinctly personal graphic style. Yet the broad and literal application of graphic elements also plays a key role in their work. They tend to opt for traditional, basic garments which they then embellish with striking patterns and motifs to give additional emphasis to their individual worlds.

Sonia Delaunay, *Blanket*, 1911

Sonia Delaunay believed that colour was a primary form of expression which enabled an artist to achieve complete abstraction. She worked intuitively whilst her solutions were constructive, and it was precisely that interaction between emotion and rationale that made her designs so special. One particular example is the appliquéd Cubist patchwork quilt that she made in 1911 for her newborn son. Seemingly carelessly, yet with an excellent sense of form and colour, the arrangement of the patches resulted in a playful, yet strongly geometric composition, and the object is now considered one of the very first completely abstract works in art history; something that in fact puts her ahead of Kandinsky and Malevich.

This seemed to be the starting point from which her later works developed, with the interaction between contrasting colours becoming increasingly essential. According to Sonia and her husband, fellow painter Robert Delaunay, colour was the only visual means of capturing both shape and movement in what they called *'simultanéisme'* (simultaneous design). In 1913, Sonia used this approach in her now iconic simultaneous dress which uses vital elements of colour, shape and rhythm. She went on to use this as the foundation for a wide range of other garments, paintings, interior design products, posters and

book covers. By doing so, she succeeded in blurring the boundaries between fine art and applied art, because in her mind, art really was inextricable from life itself. This diversity in Delaunay's products resulted in her own 'total look' that was very much based on geometric components. She continued producing graphic textile designs for customers including the company Metz & Co. well into the Sixties. Today, geometric patterns still have a surprisingly timeless quality about them whilst continuing to exemplify the 'less is more' of modernist philosophies.

Walter Van Beirendonck (1957) from Belgium, Bernhard Willhelm (1972) from Germany, Henrik Vibskov (1972) from Denmark and Bas Kosters (1977) from the Netherlands are four modern-day designers who set out, in the generations after Sonia Delaunay, to break down the barriers between life and art. Just like Delaunay, their colourful, eclectic and often carnivalesque work is the product of an open mind, but while colour still plays an important part in the expressiveness of their clothing designs, their usage of it contrasts greatly to that of the pioneering Delaunay.

The quartet's designs show audacity and faith in renewal and change; they reflect on tradition while looking ahead to a future filled with hope. There are obvious influences from popular culture, comic books and the street scene, and their interest in folklore and ethnicity, through which they manage to add a new twist to traditional designs, giving their collections freshness and, occasionally, confrontational candour. Their designs stand alone from short-lived, fleeting trends and established fashion values, yet succeed in conveying their prevailing spirit whilst simultaneously establishing connections with a variety of movements within the realm of visual art. Unexpected combinations of patterns contribute to a feeling of detachment. Their playful garments with graphic undertones frequently seem to be based on avatars that have escaped from their own universes or fantasy worlds where time does not exist.

Walter Van Beirendonck can be regarded as one of the first designers from this specific fashion movement. Covering thirty years, his oeuvre is characterised by explosions of colour, spectacular uses of materials and unexpected combinations of shapes and clothing, all independent of superficial trends. His work expresses universal topics such as friendship, love and loyalty, but major social issues with a longer expiration date also play an important part: the threat of terrorism, AIDS, hunger, overpopulation, war, censorship, gender and sexuality, excessive mass consumption and his concern for the environment are all interwoven in his collections. Yet his firm belief in progress and change enables him to express these often terrifying issues in a positive light. Tellingly, the labels on his early work carried the slogan 'Kiss the future'.

In his tongue-in-cheek, multilayered messages, Van Beirendonck mixes cute with sinister, connects innocence to repression, teams nature with culture and transforms ethnic masks into disquieting accessories. Fairy tales, aliens, spirituality, technical innovation, rituals and S&M, all fit seamlessly into the wonderful world of Walter Van Beirendonck.

He likes to play with words, and by mixing slogans, song lyrics and words into new linguistic collages which he turns into prints and embroidery, Van Beirendonck treads in the footsteps of the Surrealists. Elements that point to himself, such as the letter W and a naked doll with a beard and a penis are

Above: Walter Van Beirendonck's Walterman logo
Left: W&LT, *Wonderland*, A/W 1996–1997

Pages overleaf: catalogue for Bernhard Willhelm by Freudenthal/Verhagen, menswear A/W 2003–2004

recurring ingredients that strengthen the consistency of his graphic approach. Whether his outfits actually feature striking prints and patterns or are just plainly coloured, they always convey a total concept in which Walter Van Beirendonck's individual, highly graphic style is clearly recognisable.

Artists have created imaginary worlds in virtually every period throughout art history. And while it is easy to connect Van Beirendonck with our current era, he in fact forms part of a development that has been taking place within the arts for nearly a century.

Without wanting to over-categorise things, Bernhard Willhelm, Bas Kosters and Henrik Vibskov also appear to be part of what could be called art history's twentieth-century 'Midway' movement — falling somewhere between the 'Dionysian' and 'Apollonian' movements — which can broadly be split into two approaches: artists who use 'The Dream' as their starting point and allow their imaginations to rein free, such as the Surrealists, and artists who accept the present, passing comment on it or poking fun at it, as with Pop Art for example. Such artists generally start from the reality of the present day and involve the expression of feelings of rejection, malign or ridicule, scandal and sarcasm — often to the point of absurdity, which is exactly what Van Beirendonck, Willhelm, Kosters and Vibskov tend to do. Just like in Pop Art, they draw on the resources of their own visual culture to zoom in on everyday objects and place them in an unusual context. Surrealistic, dream-like visual art can have a similarly disorientating effect.

For Bernhard Willhelm, order and chaos, humour and horror, colourful carnival and earthy rawness go hand in hand. He looks for inspiration in what he himself calls "the power of self transformation," which often involves an element of irony, exaggeration and mockery. Graphic elements always form an essential part of his collections. Neat, straight geometric lines and checks are alternated with spontaneous, expressionist patterns that appear to be a pure coincidence. He also likes to include text and numbers in his outfits.

Willhelm uses folkloric elements in his collections that often hint at his Bavarian roots, and make it all too easy to compare him with expressive German artists such as Anselm Kiefer and the *Neue Wilden*, who also include German motifs and themes in their work. But this is not what Willhelm intended. Instead, with coincidence playing such a major part in his work, he prefers to be associated with a number of late Surrealists who wanted to switch off 'the dictator in their heads' and who saw no value in observations that were a result of the rationale. Willhelm likes to be daring and he likes to experiment. Similarly, he bases his designs on 'conceptualism' and likes to combine this with the fusion of seemingly incongruous things, an approach regularly seen in Surrealism. Such 'controlled coincidences' result in spectacular statement collections which he likes to present during 'happenings', as installations and at photo sessions. Once in the changing room, without the benefit of the scenery, set and styling, his universe seems to disappear and all you are left with is a range of contrary yet wearable garments. In that sense, Willhelm balances somewhere in between commercialism and art.

During the presentation of his graduation fashion collection 'Two teacups and a frying pan' in 2003, Bas Kosters sang a song about the items his collection was named after. Again, Kosters is another good example of a designer who merges seemingly unrelated objects effortlessly into something new, and

Bernhard Willhelm, A/W 2005–2006

Catalogue for Bernhard Willhelm by Freudenthal/Verhagen, S/S 2005

in a manner favoured by the Surrealist movement. Part of Kosters's bold visual language is cartoon-style heads with naive, happy, vacant and grim facial expressions that can be seen in his colourful prints, accessories and dolls. Initially, he regarded the world as his playground in which he could casually combine his music, painting and clothing designs. And he still does, although now, he seems to be more savvy about commercially exploiting his multiple talents: he has designed a pram for Bugaboo, for example, an underwear range for textile discounter Zeeman, and has also worked for Heineken, Kuyichi jeans and Vodafone. His work is always dotted with signs of zaniness and apparent chaos, and thanks to his use of vivid colours, hand-painted fabrics and large shapes, it is always recognisable as his, whether it's a commercial venture or not.

Unlike Van Beirendonck, Kosters does not tackle tough social issues. Instead, he prefers to broach more playful, semi-serious topics, such ridding the streets of 'frumpiness' and prejudice. With slogans on his garments that include 'Anti'(fashion), 'Can I wash my penis here?', 'Whaa', as well as his own name, he echoes the graphic approach that was so favoured by the Pop Artists. Another one of his creative initiatives is the black-and-white magazine *Extra Kak*.

Henrik Vibskov is yet another idiosyncratic, talented designer. Alongside his work as a fashion designer, he is a drummer in a band, produces films and creates fine art, usually in the form of hilarious installations. He likes to present his casual, colourful clothing lines in surrealist settings. His break-through in the Netherlands came in 2007 when he took part in the Arnhem Mode Biennale where he presented a field of boobies on sticks, components which he had used in previous shows. He manages to create a completely new vision for each of his new collections, drawing the audiences into his different imaginary worlds every time. He often uses accessories like head coverings and glasses to add to the air of mystery or quirkiness.

Vibskov's collections are based on the 'mix and match' principle. He works from an initial concept, which is usually an absurd fairy tale, and then chooses the colours, prints, materials and often traditional techniques to complement it. His first collections included colourful designs with geometric patterns for men, and he later branched out into women's fashion. These menswear and womenswear ranges are often built around a mixture of graphic elements, with busy patterns, plain sections and bold stripes all fighting for space. Thanks to his consistent approach to his garments' designs, which often sees him toying with proportions, the outfits form a cohesive whole. Since Winter 2011, his menswear range can be seen on the renowned Style.com website. This is a clear sign of recognition for his work.

Vibskov often gets invited to collaborate on other projects. In 2009, he worked with Swedish graphic designer Andreas Emenius on 'Fringe Projects' in the Zeeuws Museum in the Dutch town of Middelburg. The word 'fringe' in the title is a play on words, referring to things done out on the edge; tasks carried out on the fringe of all manner of disciplines, using various media and techniques, as well as actual fringes. The ten projects, which comprised performances, magazines, installations, videos and fashion designs, were either stand-alone exhibitions or interlinked with other aspects of the museum's collection. In one installation, the two designers were literally encased in a wall made of thousands of black-and-white fabric fringes.

Bas Kosters, *Anti Fashion Party* flyer

They were dressed in the same graphic fabric as the wall and actually became a part of the resulting relief. Another installation that was reminiscent of a car wash, complete with revolving strands of fabric, gave visitors the opportunity to enjoy their very Vibskov-esque fringe experience.

A further example of Vibskov's joint projects is the one where Dutch push-chair manufacturer and baby products label 'Quinny' persuaded Vibskov to design an innovative mother and baby collection. Needless to say, instead of using well-worn pastel colours, he spruced up carrycots, nappy bags, blankets and parasols with bold, vibrant colours and almost audibly explosive geometric patterns.

Sonia Delaunay is regarded as an artist and designer who knew how to combine 'emotion' with 'rationale'. However, few fashion designers approach their craft from these two seemingly opposing directions. In fact, she represents two other key trends that have dominated twentieth-century art: in addition to the 'Midway' movement, many artists' work is influenced by the 'Dionysian' movement, in which inner feelings or emotions serve as starting points in a similar fashion as Expressionism. Diametrically opposed is the 'Apollonian' movement in which reason has the upper hand and personal emotions are suppressed. This results in organised, impersonal art forms in which order, balance and harmony are important keywords, and can be seen in work by the likes of De Stijl artists and in computer art.

Whilst the four modern-day fashion designers discussed here seem to produce clothing that appears to be Expressionist, their strong surrealist tendencies combined with Pop Art elements imply that they actually have more in common with art history's 'Midway' movement in between 'the dream' and 'reacting to reality'. They use their garments to refer to a generally familiar context that is rooted in the present day, a context filled mainly with hope and expectation and with hardly a hint of rejection or pessimism. Their distinct visual languages help them to create their own universes in which humour and playful, childlike elements play an important role. By doing so, they create their own utopias: rooted in their imaginations, in their dreams and in the here and now, not an Apollonian, rule-based world. Feelings are also central to their creations. Although they each use graphic elements in their designs, their use of distinct visual languages gives the designs a very graphic feel too. But this is nothing new; Sonia Delaunay attracted attention with her 'poem dresses' inspired by poetry by Dada artists.

Willhelm and Kosters, and to a lesser extent Vibskov, are keen to undermine the good taste and current trends in the fashion industry. Their unconventional, often insane outfits display a unique visual language that could be called eclectic, magical, childish, carnivalesque, grotesque and imaginative. They each collaborate regularly with major labels and take part in various fashion-related projects and installations, which sometimes involves making concessions to ensure commercial success. But even this has been done before, by Delaunay. She started designing clothing in the Twenties and her work as couturier soon matched that of her contemporaries. She realised that she would need to adapt her distinct use of colours and shapes in order to succeed in the fashion industry, but thanks to her innate uniqueness, her work continued to stand out. And the same can definitely be said for Van Beirendonck, Willhelm, Kosters and Vibskov.

BIBLIOGRAPHY

Beirendonck, Walter Van, *Mutilate*, Ghent (B) 1998.

Beirendonck, Walter Van, *Dream The World Awake*, Tielt (B) 2011.

Brentjens, Yvonne, *Sonia Delaunay*, Tilburg 1988.

Damase, Jacques, *Sonia Delaunay, Fashion and fabrics*, London 1991.

Townsend, Chris, 'Slave to the rhythm, Sonia Delaunay's fashion project and the fragmentary, mobile modernist body', in: Jan Brand and José Teunissen, *The power of fashion, About design and meaning*, Arnhem 2006.

Verhagen, Kirsten, a.o. (eds.), *Bernhard Willhelm & Jutta Kraus*, Groningen/Rotterdam 2009.

Zidianakis, Vassilis (ed.), *Not a toy, fashioning radical characters*, Berlin 2011.

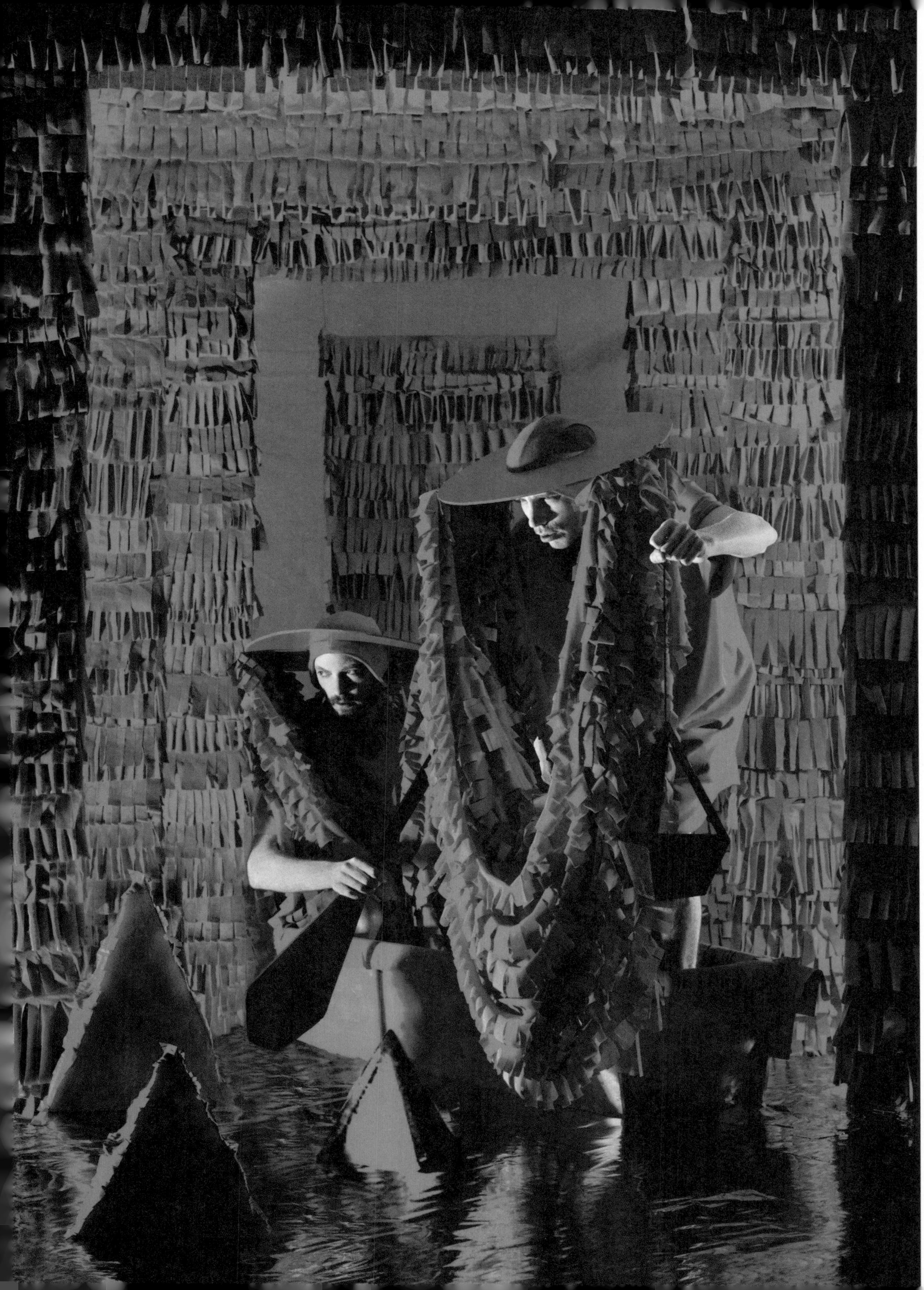

Vibskov & Emenius, *Fringe Project 6*, 2008

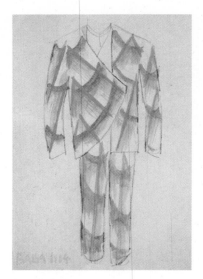

Giacomo Balla, *Morning*,
designs for a men's suit, 1914

While the Reform Movement and the Wiener Werkstätte cast a nostalgic gaze on the past and detested the modern era with its industrial means of production and rapid changes, this very modernity was enthusiastically welcomed by the Futurists. Futurism was launched by the Italian poet, writer and journalist Filippo Tomasso Marinetti (1876–1944) whose *Futurist Manifesto* was published on the front page of the French newspaper *Le Figaro* in February 1909. A year later appeared the Manifesto of Futurist Painters signed by, among others, Umberto Boccioni, Carlo Carrà and Giacomo Balla. Like a number of nineteenth-century art movements, the Futurists wanted to abolish the boundaries between life and art. Marinetti and his companions were striving for an *artecrazia*, a rule of art which meant that the existing bourgeois society had to be utterly changed. War, which according to Marinetti was "the world's only hygiene," could be an excellent aid in accomplishing this since it could sweep away the ballast of the past. He advocated the demolition of museums and libraries, seeing tradition as a brake on progress and thus on life itself. Freedom, originality, modern technology, speed, progress, dynamism, the big city — these are all notions that were at the centre of the vocabulary of the Futurists who firmly believed in the new times and in human potential.

It almost goes without saying that clothing, as one of the representatives of bourgeois culture, could not be excluded from the great social revolution that the Futurists envisaged. In 1911, Arnaldo Cinna and Bruno Corra were already vehemently complaining

about the major manufacturers of women's fashion, which in their eyes were responsible for the many mismatched colours and silhouettes that determined the street scene. Volt (pseudonym of Vincenzo Fani) was of the opinion that clothing was so important that in his 1920 *Manifesto della moda femminile futurista* he advocated the appointment of important poets and painters as directors of major fashion houses. A well-designed dress worn in the correct manner was in his eyes just as valuable as a Michelangelo fresco or a Titian Madonna.

It is striking, but at the same time completely logical, that Futurism focused mainly on men's clothing, while earlier movements to change fashion had concentrated on women's clothing. After all, women's clothing, under the influence of fashion, was completely irrational and subject to constant change, new ideas and unbridled creativity. In the words of Volt, it was thus already 'more or less Futurist'. Men's clothing, on the other hand, was rational and stable and an expression of such supremely bourgeois values as frugality, uprightness and respectability. And according to the Futurists, who strived for permanent change and had a predilection for risks and danger, it was precisely there that the problem lay. In addition, femininity was associated with weakness and the past, masculinity with strength and progress. And this progress was what the Futurists were after.

In his *Manifesto futurista del vestito da uomo* published in 1914, Giacomo Balla (1871–1958), often regarded as the father of Futurist fashion, argued that for centuries European streets, theatres and salons

CLOTHING & FUTURISM

BALLA 1914

had presented a cheerless, funereal aspect because of the dark, rigid and ill-fitting men's clothing. In his view this mainly backward-looking clothing constricted and hindered, and hence in fact denied, the muscular male body. Furthermore, the black fabrics did not breathe and were therefore unhygienic, and the frequently used halftones boring, feminine or even decadent; all in all, reason enough for Balla to propose radically different men's clothing — clothing that should rejuvenate people in the street and liberate them from the apparently heavy burden of life.

To start with, he wanted to ban a number of characteristics of men's clothing once and for all. Mourning attire, as far as he was concerned, should disappear, and likewise bleached, neutral and dark colours. The same went for striped and chequered fabrics and fabrics with dots. Other things that he no longer wanted to see were unnecessary buttons, starched collars and cuffs and symmetrical designs. Balla did, however, offer something in exchange. The Futurist clothing he had in mind exuded a dynamism with its merry, bright, possibly even fluorescent colours, and idiosyncratic patterns — preferably triangles, circles, cones, ellipses and spirals. A preference which, as it happened, evidenced a strong relationship with Cubism. This clothing furthermore, had to be asymmetrical, simple and comfortable, hygienic and able to breathe. A short life was also important, so that there would always be something new to enjoy. But perhaps the most important demand was that Futurist clothing should be variable. All manner of accessories in different widths and colours, which could be applied

at will, meant that the dreamed-of Futurist men's suit could be adapted to the mood of the wearer. The suit could thus be flattering in appearance but also shocking, diplomatic, commanding or resolute. The ultimate example of such a variable accessory was the Futurist necktie which Balla had made for his own use and which incorporated a light bulb. It was connected to a battery so that he could switch it on at important moments during his speeches so as to underline and enhance his arguments. Clothing had hence become a form of self-expression as never before, and the wearer of the clothing was transformed into a provocateur and stage artist.

According to Balla, the new clothing would quickly give a very different look to the cities, even if the inhabitants were lacking in fantasy and a feeling for colour. The city, which by that time would undoubtedly be designed wholly in the Futurist style, would begin to sparkle and glitter like the shop window of a jeweller. However, it would never come this far. Balla did manage to get some of his designs manufactured by a local tailor or in his own studio by one of his daughters, but large-scale production was out of the question. Futurist fashion was and remained more theory than practice. The reactions of the public to the creations that were actually realized were not always positive. The story goes that Balla had visited the Art Deco exhibition in Paris in 1925 but was unable to find a place to sleep afterwards. He had tried no fewer than thirty-one hotels, but each time he arrived at the reception desk in his Futuristic outfit the hotel was suddenly fully booked.

Giacomo Balla, house costume,
worn by himself, 1925

A much more sober Futurist was Ernesto Thayaht (pseudonym of Ernesto Michahelles), who was mainly known for his 'tuta', a one-piece garment which was clearly related to the American overall and, unusual for a Futurist, unchangeable. It was an attempt at eroding the notion of fashion in a very different way. 'Tuta' was a play on words based on the Italian word 'tutta' meaning 'everything', thus referring to all the occasions for which the garment was suitable. The missing T reappeared in the pattern itself — when flat it took on precisely the form of that letter. Thayaht had designed a tuta for both men and women, both of them convenient and comfortable and without any gaudery or decoration. This radical austerity, however, did not prevent him from designing very elegant evening dresses for Madeleine Vionnet a few years later.

In the Twenties, Giacomo Balla, the designer who wanted to give the men's suit such a different look, went on to design mainly women's clothing, usually for his two daughters. As far as men's clothing was concerned, the torch was handed on to, among others, Tullio Crali (1910–2000), a second-generation Futurist who designed, for himself, asymmetrical jackets without collars, or with just a left-hand collar in a colour that sharply contrasted with the rest of the jacket. An accompanying shirt was fixed at the neck with a cufflink. A tie, on the other hand, was totally unsuitable. Despite the many Futurist designs for ties and the fact that even a special manifesto was devoted to them, Crali regarded the tie as a traditional item of clothing that should disappear as quickly as possible.

Crali also went on to design clothing for women, taking no account at all of production or wearability. He fully indulged himself in sketches of dynamic spirals, triangles and other forms that folded themselves around the body and were held together as though by a miracle.

Futurism often appeared in a bad light in post-1945 Europe. The Futurists, after all, had been closely connected with Italian fascism, and Marinetti was even one of the founders of the Fasci di combattimento in 1919. Certain fascist ideals — think for example of the muscular male body and the love of the fatherland — corresponded strongly with those of Futurism. There was also a Futurist men's suit in the colours of the Italian flag, which was worn during a student demonstration against the neutral professors who wanted to keep Italy out of the First World War. And one of the Futurist manifestos, *Il manifesto futurista del capella italiano*, was not only a plea for wearing a hat in the Italian manner, but at the same time an unadulterated nationalistic ode to the Italian style and the Italian race. Yet Futurism was also rebellious, non-conformist, emancipatory, autonomous and sometimes even oriented towards the radical left, so it certainly cannot be dismissed as a simple extension of fascism. The Futurists also advocated the use of cheap materials and insisted that good designs be made accessible to everyone, which meant that they led the way in the later democratisation of fashion, when style was no longer reserved for the moneyed class. That this style would become more and more elegant, more Italian in other words, is something that the Futurists would

Giacomo Balla, knitwear design, ca. 1930

Tulio Crali, design for a dress, 1932

have been pleased to hear. But perhaps their most important contribution to the fashion climate is that they no longer regarded clothing as merely something to cover the body with, but acknowledged it as a performance, as an extension of one's personality, as a way to show who you are and what you stand for.

BIBLIOGRAPHY

Emily Braun, 'Futurist fashion: three manifestoes', *Art Journal*, 54 (1995), nr. 1.

Günter Berghaus, *Futurism and politics. Between anarchist rebellion and fascist reaction, 1909–1944*: Berghahn Books, Oxford/New York, 1995.

Arnold Heumakers, 'Leve de machines. Politieke studie over het futurisme', *NRC Handelsblad*, 31 January 1997.

Radu Stern, *Gegen den Strich. Kleider von Künstlern. Vêtements d'artistes 1900–1940*, Benteli Verlag, Bern 1992.

The colourful and chaotic world of multitalented Bas Kosters (1977) knows no bounds. Kosters graduated from Enschede's AKI in 2001 with his extravagant 'Dumpster Queens' collection. He subsequently studied for his master's degree at the Fashion Institute Arnhem, where he successfully presented his graduation project 'Two Teacups and a Frying Pan' in 2003, a collection containing many references to surrealism, which also earned him the jury prize in the Robijn Fashion Awards that same year. For Bas Kosters, it's not enough to simply reveal his collection during a catwalk show; he much prefers to combine fashion with music and theatre. In his graduation collection for the FIA, *Two Teacups and a Frying Pan*, his distinctive approach was visible in an over-the-top pop concert in which he himself performed with his band, Bas Und Sein Verrucktes Musikanten Stadle. In 2005, Bas Kosters launched his own label called Bas Kosters Studio.

Kosters's work typically features a multidisciplinary approach; it allows him to create an entirely self-contained universe in which gender, race, religion and political beliefs are irrelevant — everyone is welcome. The way he presents his collections underlines this fact: instead of selecting professionals to model his garments, he prefers to invite a cross-section of his friends and acquaintances to strut his catwalks — whether young or old, fat or thin, male, female or transgender. Another example of this open-mindedness is the Anti-Fashion Party, which Kosters organises twice a year. Representing much more than just a party, this event offers a platform for like-minded designers, musicians, artists and performers to present their work to the public in a spirit of openness and acceptance. Another platform Kosters has created is the *Extra Kak Magazine*, which appeared for the first time in December 2011. This publication allows Bas Kosters to share his vision and sources of inspiration through collages and illustrations: "non-shiny, copy style, black and white, A4," as he himself puts it. A prominent role is reserved in the magazines for Bas Kosters's dolls, which have appeared — in all shapes and sizes — in each of his works since the start of his career, and form an essential part of his brand identity. Kosters: "These dolls play a key role in my work, and feature in all manner of ways, including in prints on my garments. This multidisciplinary approach reinforces the way my clothing is positioned and communicated, and produces a compact, clearly recognisable and 'in-your-face' visual language."[1]

In addition to the simple, almost childlike black-and-white drawings of dolls that regularly appear as prints on garments and other Bas Kosters products, his visual style is also characterised by vibrant colours, hand-painted fabrics and cheeky slogans such as: 'Can I wash my penis here?' and 'That puts the u in ugly'. Such typical Kosters elements work together to create a 'total look' with which the designer creates his own universe. To extend that universe even further, Kosters is happy to collaborate with major commercial partners such as textile discounter Zeeman, Heineken, Kuyichi jeans, Vodafone and Bugaboo. Bas Kosters: "While fashion is a common theme running through my work, my design activities don't always have to be aimed at producing clothing collections."[2]

www.baskosters.com

Invitation for Bas Kosters, *Red Carpet*, A/W 2007–2008

1 http://www.ccaa.nl/page/9382/nl.

2 http://www.parool.nl/parool/nl/12/CULTUUR/article/detail/277786/2010/02/02/Fong-Leng-ontmoet-Bas-Kosters.dhtml.

Top: Bas Kosters for Heineken,
Heineken's beat collection, 2009
Right: backstage at Bas Kosters,
12Tree, A/W 2012–2013

Bas Kosters, *Two Teacups and a Frying Pan*, 2003

Bas Kosters, *Extra Kak Magazine #1 and #3*, 2011

The Danish fashion designer Henrik Vibskov does not like to be pigeonholed. Besides designing four collections a year for both men and women, Vibskov plays drums in electronic musician Trentemøller's live band and is part of 'The Fringe Project', together with visual artist Andreas Emenius. Everything Henrik Vibskov does has only one goal: to create his own surreal universe in which the sky is the limit. Vibskov is a true romantic at heart: he only applied for the fashion design course at Central Saint Martins because a girl he had his eye on was doing so too.

Vibskov finds his inspiration in Nordic folk traditions and childhood memories of his hometown in Jutland, Denmark. But it is never just about the clothes with Henrik Vibskov; to present his collections, he creates extravagant narratives, filling catwalks with bicycles, wooden boats, shiny boobies, humongous hamster wheels and black carrots, like a little boy's fantasy that has come to life. His style is best described as whimsical and quirky, with show titles such as: 'The Fantabulous Bicycle Music Factory' (S/S 2008), 'The Human Laundry Service' (A/W 2009–2010) and 'The Last Pier Pandemonium' (S/S 2011) that sound like Roald Dahl stories. Henrik Vibskov's world looks like it is made of Lego but his colourful designs never stop being wearable, and they never completely lose touch with reality.

www.henrikvibskov.com

Henrik Vibskov, *The Shrink Wrap Spectacular*, Paris 2012

Henrik Vibskov for Quinny, 2008

Henrik Bibskov, Zurich Knit, *The Solar Donkey Experiment*, S/S 2010

Belgian fashion designer Walter Van Beirendonck (1957) is regarded as a defining figure within Belgian fashion culture. The joint show organised during the London Designer Show in 1980 by the 'Antwerp Six', which comprised Walter Van Beirendonck, Dirk Bikkembergs, Ann Demeulemeester, Dirk Van Saene, Dries Van Noten and Marina Yee, firmly put Antwerp on the international fashion map. Van Beirendonck graduated from the city's Royal Academy of Fine Arts in 1983 returning two years later as a lecturer. In 2006, he became head of the Academy's fashion department.

Van Beirendonck is the most extravagant of the 'Antwerp Six', characterised by his highly visual, emotionally stimulating creations that stem from a unique fairy-tale world located inside his head. His collections feature striking graphic prints and a specific use of colour that is combined with absurd silhouettes, a touch of humour and a positive vibe. Yet the work of this 'aesthetic terrorist' is also interwoven with references to social issues such as AIDS, gender, terrorism, the environment, mass consumerism and the commercial side of the very fashion industry of which he too forms a part. These he counterbalances with themes like friendship and love. His interpretation is pure, almost naive, as he puts society's problems in a dreamlike context. Van Beirendonck's creative spirit feeds on all manner of ideas from ethnic tribes such as the Maya, Zulu and Papuan peoples to American superheroes and avatars, but he also draws inspiration from current affairs, films, pop music and politics. He uses his spectacular fashion shows in Paris and his new collections as a way of telling his latest story to the international fashion world. Notably, he chooses to present his clothing on 'real people' rather than models who embody the traditional ideals of the fashion industry.

In contrast to what one might assume from his theatrical, dreamlike fashion shows, the last thing on Van Beirendonck's mind is entertainment. With his confrontational style, he endeavours to make people reflect, while staying one step ahead of fashion hypes. His labels, since 1983, have included Walter Van Beirendonck and Walter Worldwide, W&LT (1993–1999) and Æstheticterrorists by Walter (1999–2004). He was artistic director of Scapa Sports and the children's label ZulupaPUWA belonging to JBC. He has launched a shoe line for W6YZ and, in 1998, he opened his flagship store annex gallery 'Walter®' in Antwerp, although this was recently forced to move to a different location and scale down, due to the current economic climate. Furthermore, Van Beirendonck is involved in designing costumes for the world of theatre, ballet, film and pop music, illustrating books, and as curator of various exhibitions in the MoMu.

www.waltervanbeirendonck.com

Walter Van Beirendonck, *Wonder*, S/S 2010

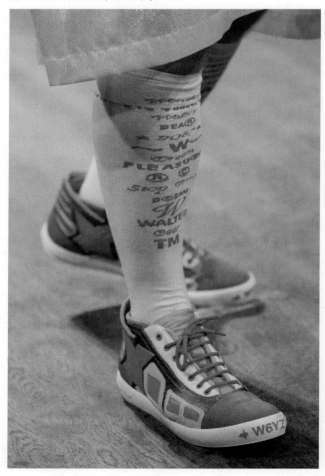

Walter Van Beirendonck
'eXplicit'

FIRENZE

**PITTI IMMAGINE
MENSWEAR SHOW
SUMMER COLLECTION 2009
THURSDAY JUNE 19TH 2008
6:30 PM
GIARDINO DEL MUSEO STIBBERT
VIA FREDERICK STIBBERT, 26
FIRENZE**

FONDAZIONE PITTI DISCOVERY

**PRESS CONTACT: KUKI DE SALVERTES | TOTEM
SEBASTIEN@TOTEMFASHION.COM
STEPHANIE@TOTEMFASHION.COM
TEL. +33 1 49 23 79 79**

WWW.WALTERVANBEIRENDONCK.COM

PARIS

**SHOWROOM
SUMMER COLLECTION 2009
27, 28, 29 & 30 JUNE 2008
GALERIE VERDIER
3, RUE SAINT-CLAUDE
75003 PARIS
TEL. +33 (0)952 83 75 86
FAX +33 1 42 74 06 70
METRO: ST.-SÉBASTIEN FROISSART**

**FOR ALL APPOINTMENTS PLEASE CONTACT BVBA BIG:
HENRI VAN HEURCKSTRAAT 5
2000 ANTWERP BELGIUM
TEL. +32 (0)3 231 77 32 | FAX +32 (0)3 233 27 13
BIGBVBA@SKYNET.BE | MOBILE +32 (0)486 82 27 60**

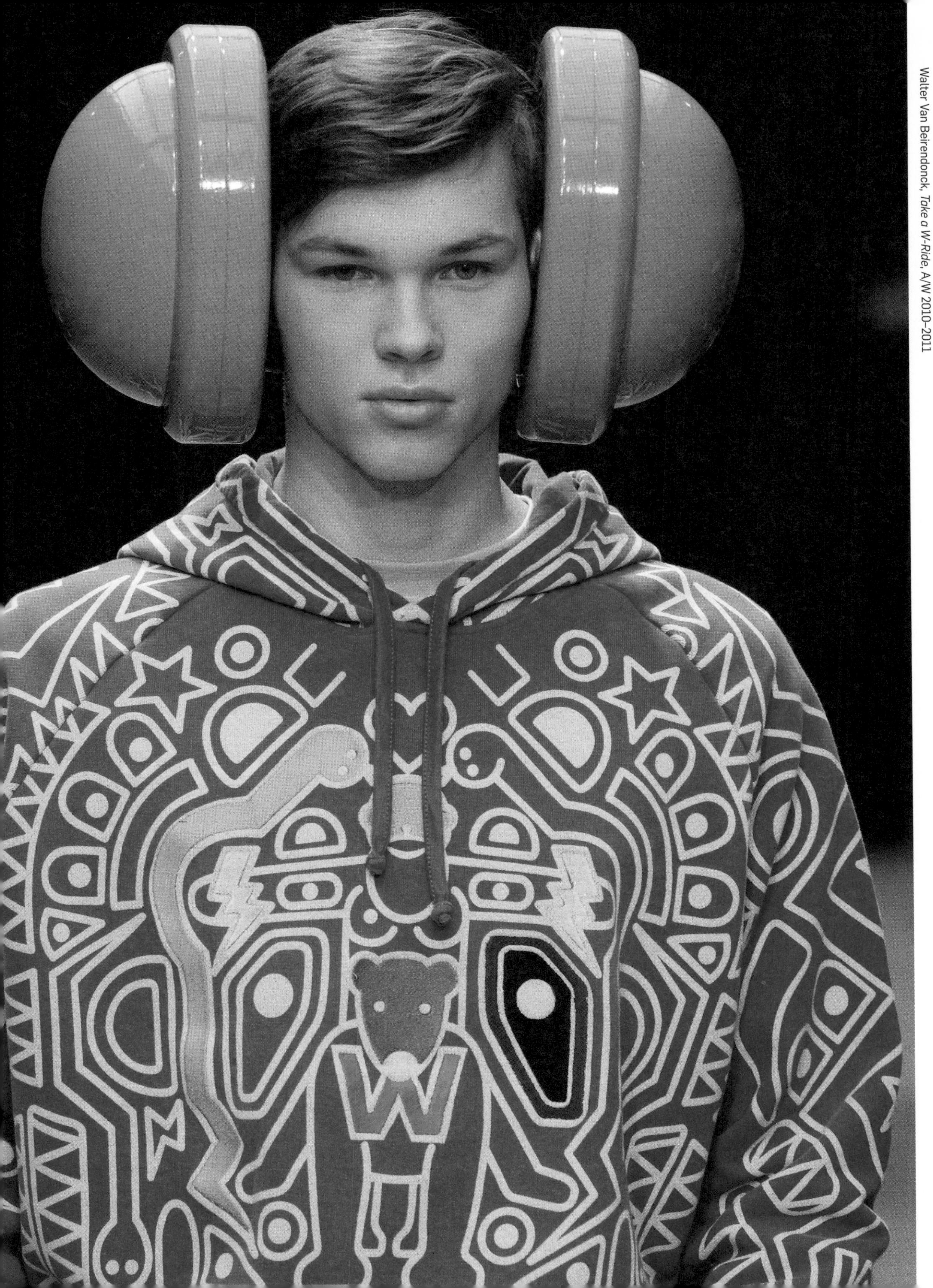

Walter Van Beirendonck, *Take a W-Ride*, A/W 2010–2011

'Alice in Wonderland' and 'Black is also available in white' are both working titles by the German fashion duo Bernhard Willhelm (1972) and Jutta Kraus (1972); titles that, whilst saying so very much and so very little at the same time, perfectly reflect just how difficult it is to describe the duo's design philosophies.

Willhelm and Kraus have been shaping the Bernhard Willhelm label together since 1999. What the label strives to do is bypass the proportions and contours of fashion as we know it. It is a mixture of images, iconography, clashing colours, contrasting patterns and styles resulting in collections that are visual explosions. The all-encompassing artistic approach, visual paradoxes and plays on words, and an 'aesthetic barbarism' are all typical of the Bernhard Willhelm label.

Bernhard Willhelm's childhood provides some degree of insight into the wonderful world of his imagination. He grew up in Bavaria, the home of Grimm's fairy tales, the Black Forest and unspoilt nature. As a child he was fascinated by biology and botany and he loved looking at the world through his microscope. While these elements can be found in his fashion collections, his Bavarian roots are also suppressed by

images that are actually at odds with what you think you comprehend. Ghosts, yodelling broomsticks, images of pop stars, commercial logos, signage tape — absolutely anything imaginable, by coincidence and through pure intuition.

In an interview with Dutch newspaper *NRC Handelsblad* in 2007 , Willhelm explains that, for him, "fashion is a creative craft, just like art. I thrive on a certain amount of chaos. Nothing ages quite as quickly as minimalism."

Bernhard Willhelm's fashion shows in Paris also go against the grain of the normal catwalk event. They are artistic fashion 'happenings' ranging from video clips to tableaux vivants, often produced with help from photographers and multimedia artists he is acquainted with, that involve everyone and no one in 'the moment'. They are more like exhibits that involve the audience whilst excluding them at the same time. People can walk past, around and through the presentation, making contact with the models who in turn, play their own isolated roles in these avant-garde 'Gesamtkunstwerken'.

Kraus and Willhelm's outspoken style is characterised by its use of contradictions and paradoxes. It transcends the postmodernism which puts it in the realms of meta-modern fashion.

Bernhard Willhelm graduated from Antwerp's Royal Academy of Fine Arts in 1998, was an intern for Walter Van Beirendonck and collaborated with Vivienne Westwood, Dirk Bikkembergs and Alexander McQueen. In addition to women's fashion, he started designing menswear collections in 2003, mainly to challenge the boundaries of fashion in that area too.
In 2006, the Bernhard Willhelm label opened a flagship store in Tokyo. From their home in Paris, Willhelm and Kraus regularly work with pop stars such as Björk, and are also involved with the art direction for the Capucci fashion house.

www.bernhard-willhelm.com

Catalogue for Bernhard Willhelm by Freudenthal/Verhagen, menswear A/W 2005–2006

In line with his philosophy of 'Turn your frown upside down', Dutch fashion designer Antoine Peters (1981) creates cheerful, narrative and tactile collections with a pop art message.

The Antoine Peters label stands for optimism and surrealism. His breezy concepts put serious issues in a positive light. He applies graphic design techniques, blows up his prints until they become distorted or take on new meanings, and uses the simplicity of denim, T-shirts and jumpers as a foundation for all of his collections.

In 2004, Antoine Peters graduated cum laude in Fashion Design from the ArtEZ Institute of the Arts and completed his master's degree two years later at the Fashion Institute Arnhem. Even while he was an undergraduate, his designs would attract attention thanks to his use of graphic design, his ability to tell stories and his parodies on society, with the latter also echoing in the names of his collections. In 'Looking ridiculous in the company of fools', his graduation collection in 2004, he captured Paris Hilton-style 'shop-aholicism' in voluminous skirts made of shopping bags, tangled garments, buttons and broken hearts. He achieved his breakthrough with an interactive project 'A sweater for the world!' in 2006 which was a jumper made for two people, designed with the aim of bringing as many different individuals together as possible, in order to challenge people's intolerances. During the Amsterdam Fashion Week in 2008, he presented his debut collection 'Le Petit Antoine' (S/S 2008) in which his infectious naivety, illustrative graphic style and his fascination with transformation shone through.

Mass culture and pop art represent key sources of inspiration for his humorous themes. Often bordering on the farcical, these counterbalance the gravity and melancholy that he sees around him, in music, literature and the media. Antoine Peters's designs form a continual narrative and he himself regards fashion as a means of visual communication. Antoine: "I magnify images in order to grab people's attention, but if you look more closely, there is more to my designs. I create multiple layers at the micro level and to me, these represent the interdisciplinary nature of fashion. Fashion enables you to tell the whole story using unusual seams, the grain of the fabric, the lines, the materials, the prints, the shapes; they all play a part in my themes and I carry this through to the smallest of details, from the smiley stitched into the label at the back of the neck to the typography on my invitations."

Together with his partner and graphic designer Karen van de Kraats, he has developed his 'Petit Antoines' into an all-encompassing theme that has become an integral part of his collection and his art direction. Antoine collaborates regularly with commercial fashion brands that have an affinity with his upbeat philosophy, including United Nude, Eastpak, Quinze & Milan, EFFIO and GSUS, and he has also worked on a number of special projects such as Fur Free Fashion ('Crying Furcoat', 2011), Arnhem Mode Biennale (the volunteers' costumes for the Arnhem Fashion Biennale 2009), KesselsKramer Outlet London ('Knickers Dress', 2011), Krause (Arrow Dress, 2011) and he designed the dancers' costumes for the Introdans 'For Life' choreography in 2007.

www.antoinepeters.com

Left: Antoine Peters's label; *Turn your frown upside down*, S/S 2010
Top right: Antoine Peters, *The world is flat*, S/S 2011
Below left: *Fat people are harder to kidnap*, A/W 2008–2009
Below right: *Happy Burka* T-shirt, S/S 2008

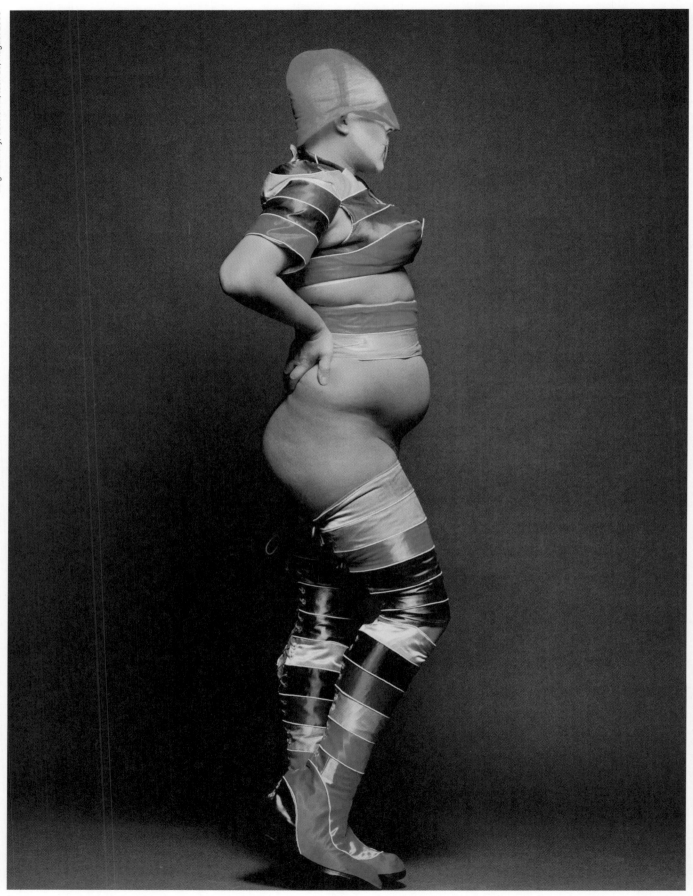

Leigh Bowery, Session III, look 15, August 1990

Australian-born Leigh Bowery (1961–1994) was a man of extremes. Living and working in London from 1980 onwards, he both embraced and embodied the art of exaggeration in the way he presented himself. He created a new work of art every day using himself as a canvas for his self-designed costumes and make-up that went beyond the realms of the imagination. He appeared in public decked in glitter, duct tape, body paint, platform shoes or enormous latex body suits that covered him from head to toe. Both his style and his lifestyle ensured that he left his mark on the New Wave movement of the Eighties and Nineties. His jobs included working as an actor, club promoter, model, tailor, artist and later owner of the Taboo nightclub, the Studio 54 of London. He didn't care what he did, as long as he was the centre of attention.

During his short life, Bowery was an exhibitionist, a narcissist and a favourite of the international avant-garde. While he was not renowned as a fashion designer, Bowery presented several of his collections in New York, Tokyo and at London Fashion Week. He would seek confrontation through his outfits and extremely high-heeled shoes, which added extra height to his imposing stature. He made an unforgettable impression on anyone who cast eyes on him in the street or in the clubs with his bizarre, disturbing, clown-like, vibrant and out-of-this-world costumes. From an artistic viewpoint, it was laudable how he transformed himself into real-life works of art day after day. In 1988, for example, he spent a week reclining on a chaise longue in the showroom of Anthony d'Offay's prestigious Dering Street Gallery dressed in a variety of outfits and surrounded by mirrors.

Perhaps unexpectedly, Bowery did not generate a significant level of income from the way he dressed, nor did he receive royalties from the countless images of him that were in circulation. As he put it: "I have a profile, but I have no money." Instead, artistes like Bowery lived off charitable donations and sought refuge in the mysterious underworld of homo-erotic nightclubs. However, during a performance in 1993, Bowery crossed the line with an S&M act in a Nazi uniform, signalling the end of his cult status. For a while, it seemed he might be making a comeback with his band Minty, but that turned out to be a financial flop: the Minty show was banned after just one night.

In 1994, Bowery died of an AIDS-related illness, but his out-of-this-world, unisex outfits with which he pushed back the boundaries of colour, texture, shape and fabric still continue to inspire modern-day fashion designers. His style has clearly influenced the work of designers such as Gareth Pugh, Alexander McQueen and John Galliano, artistes including Björk, Lady Gaga and the Scissor Sisters, multimedia artist Matthew Barney, photographer David LaChapelle, and even Tokyo's Harajuku street fashion. Boy George dedicated his track 'Satan's Butterfly Ball' to Bowery in 1995. In 2002, Charles Atlas released the documentary *The Legend of Leigh Bowery*.

Leigh Bowery, Session IV, look 17, August 1991

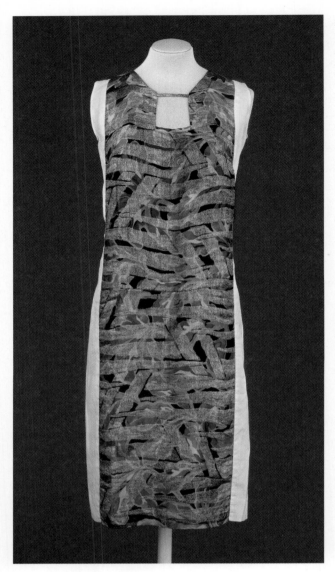

Sonia Delaunay dress, 1925–1928

The Paris-based Ukrainian-French painter Sonia Delaunay-Terk (1885–1979) became known as a textile designer thanks, primarily, to her futuristic, intellectual vision of clothing. To her mind, there was no distinction between art, the body and life.

Just as she had done in her paintings from 1905, she began experimenting on fabrics with bold colours, a sense of rhythm and geometric shapes, creating a vibrancy that reflected her take on life in contemporary Paris which was in the throes of industrialisation.[1] It was a time of optimism, new mobility, technological advancement and urban life that was lived largely outside and revolved around motor cars, cycling, parties and other outdoor pursuits. This required a new interpretation of clothing, just as cubism and futurism — styles that she drew inspiration from — had created a new visual language in the world of art. At that time, it was unheard of that clothing could come so close to being a wearable work of art, as the displays on her garments were. Her creations were actually worn by a small, international group of avant-garde admirers which included Hollywood actress Gloria Swanson. Sonia Delaunay's graphic approach was comparable to that of a director. Even before art direction existed as a concept, she was creating total experiences in which design, emotion and context were closely interlinked. In that sense, she was way ahead of her time. Furthermore, her bold, graphic patterns were radically different from what her contemporaries such as Paul Poiret and, later, Gabrielle Coco Chanel were doing. But above all, rather than being a glamorous fashion designer, she was an artist through and through.

Sonia Delaunay experienced her glory years in the first quarter of the twentieth century; she had several outlets in Spain and Paris and exhibited during the World Exhibition of 1925. However, the 1929 depression caused her to go bankrupt, spelling the end for her clothing creations.[2] She continued to work as an artist in Paris until her death in 1979.

We see echoes of her unique, graphic take on fashion, her distinct language of shapes, her reliance on intuition and her art-direction style, not only in modern-day designs by Bas Kosters, Antoine Peters, Walter Van Beirendonck and Bernhard Willhelm[3], but also in the work of twentieth-century artists such as Piet Mondriaan, Keith Haring and Andy Warhol, all of whom took their artistic visions to extremes in their art and in their lives.

1 Seeling, Charlotte, *Mode. De eeuw van de ontwerpers 1900–1999*, Publisher: Konemann (Dutch edition) 2000, p. 302.

2 Jan Brand and José Teunissen (eds.), *De Macht van Mode*, Terra Lannoo 2009, p. 233.

3 See also Els de Baan's article in this book.

Dries Van Noten, A/W 2012–013

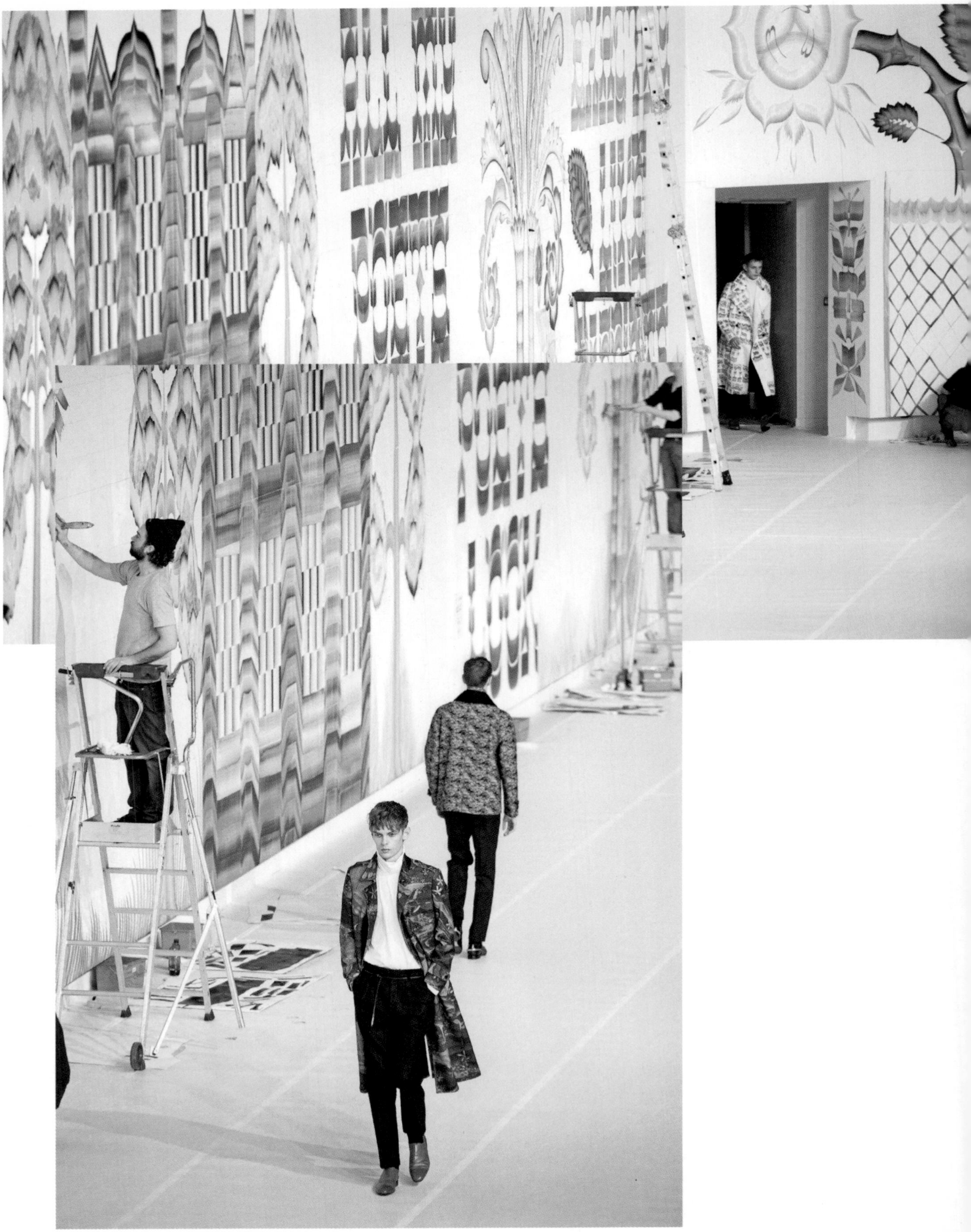

Belgian designer Dries Van Noten (1958) launched his eponymous label in 1986, six years after graduating from Antwerp's Royal Academy of Fine Arts. Van Noten was a member of the 'Antwerp Six', the group of young Belgian designers who took fashion in a radically new direction in the Eighties.

Dries Van Noten's designs are classic, with a primary focus on wearability, and are known for their extravagant, often ethnic prints and intricate embroidery. Particularly striking is his A/W 2012–2013 menswear collection, which he produced in collaboration with Dutch artist Gijs Frieling and graphic designer Job Wouters. Van Noten came across their work in the book entitled *Vernacular Painting* (Valiz, 2009) about Frieling's murals which juxtapose folkloric influences with Christian iconography. When developing the book's typography, Job Wouters used the two-tone brush technique favoured by Frieling in his murals as the basis for creating a new font. In addition to using a number of prints from the book, which he chose based on their ornateness, Dries Van Noten also commissioned Frieling and Wouters to design several new ones. He then combined the colourful prints with his restrained, almost Victorian-style garment designs, resulting in what Van Noten himself described as "psychedelic elegance."

Gijs Frieling and Job Wouters also formed part of the show itself, which was held in the Grand Palais in Paris. For the duration of the event, the pair, helped by four assistants, could be seen painting a mural measuring some fifty metres wide and five metres high, while models walked up and down the catwalk to the sound of Frank Zappa's music and the narration of Oscar Wilde's *The Happy Prince*. A total of twenty-four hours of work went into completing the mural.

www.driesvannoten.be

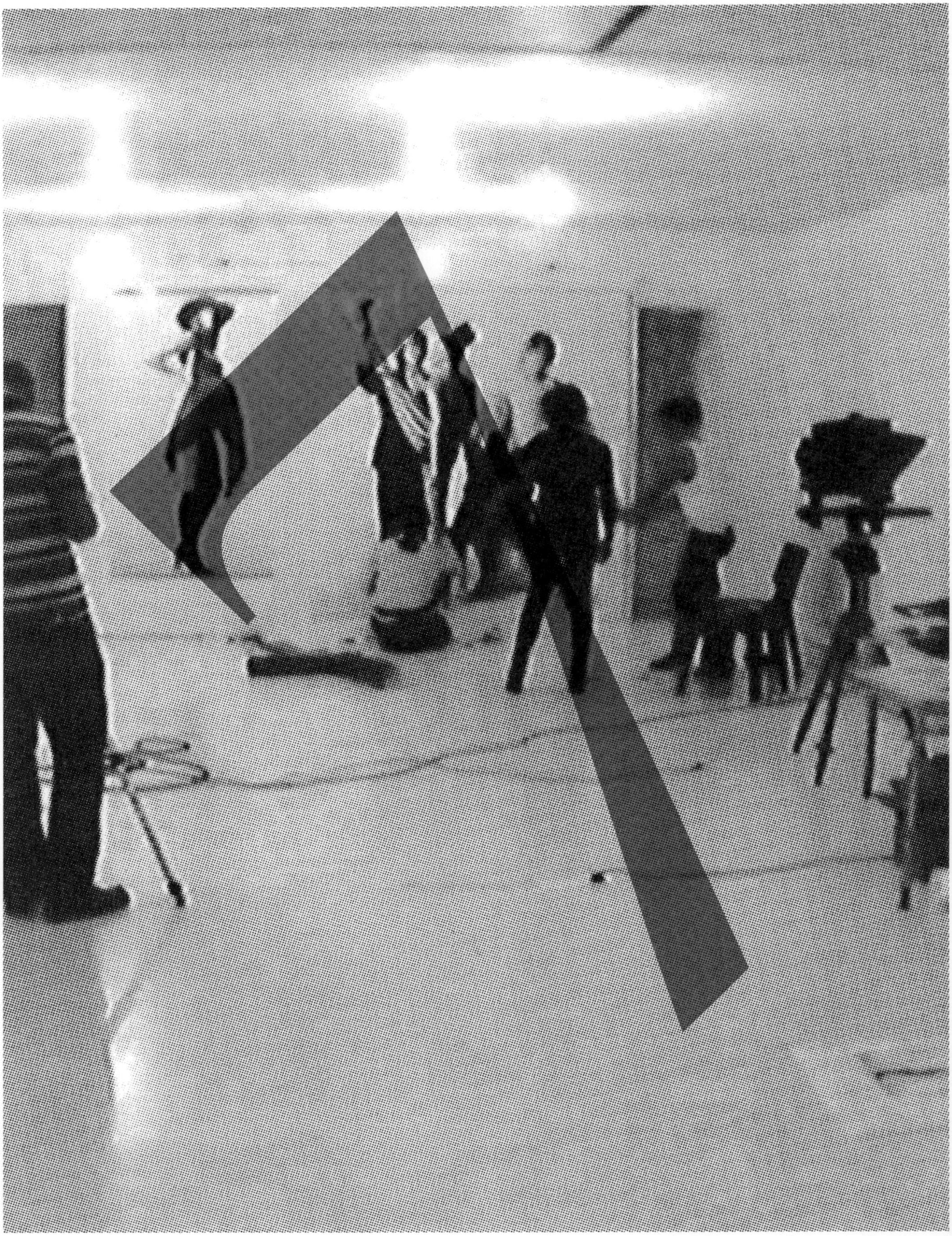

SHOWstudio's studio space, live webcam image, April 2004

FASHION & FILM: A POWER SHIFT

— HANKA VAN DER VOET

David Lynch did it for Gucci, Martin Scorsese for Chanel and Sofia Coppola for Dior: directing a commercial. Leading Hollywood directors are not the only ones increasingly lending their talents to capturing a brand's visual identity in a short film — many fashion photographers are moving into films too. The short film directed by Steven Meisel, in-house photographer at *Vogue Italia* and fashion label Prada, for Prada's S/S 2011 collection was a huge hit on the internet. Photographers such as Nick Knight, Inez van Lamsweerde & Vinoodh Matadin regularly produce short fashion films. This should come as no surprise, since fashion is at its best when it's seen in motion, as countless movies have demonstrated: Audrey Hepburn's stylish Givenchy wardrobe in *Breakfast at Tiffany's* (1961), Richard Gere's masculine Giorgio Armani suits in *American Gigolo* (1980) and the numerous Yves Saint Laurent ensembles worn by Catherine Deneuve in films like *Belle de Jour* (1967), *La Chamade* (1968), *Mississippi Mermaid* (1969), *Liza* (1972), *Un flic* (1972) and *The Hunger* (1983). The fashion documentary has also become more popular in recent years. *Lagerfeld Confidential* (2007), for instance, offers an insight into the fascinating life of Chanel designer Karl Lagerfeld, and *Valentino: The Last Emperor* (2008) follows couturier Valentino Garavani in his final days at his fashion house's helm. Clearly, the fashion film — whatever its length — is a genre that deserves to be taken seriously. But why is this explosion of fashion films occurring right now? Why are increasing numbers of designers opting for a short fashion film as the vehicle for presenting their new collections? And what role are social media and broadband internet playing in this development?

For many years, the catwalk show was regarded as a designer's ultimate means of expression, especially after Thierry Mugler unleashed its potential in the Eighties. For his A/W 1984–1985 collection catwalk show, Mugler spent a million dollars on re-enacting the birth of Jesus Christ. He also believed that the catwalk show should be accessible to everyone, rather than just a select group of fashionistas. As long as their pockets were deep enough, anyone could purchase a ticket for a Thierry Mugler extravaganza. As a result, both he and John Galliano, who later organised similarly spectacular events, attracted criticism for substituting theatre for fashion and allowing the shows to overshadow the clothes.[1] After the launch of *SHOWstudio.com* in 2000,

1 Caroline Evans, *Fashion at the Edge: Spectacle, Modernity and Deathliness*, Yale University Press 2003, p. 69.

the power of the catwalk, and also of the fashion magazine, was increasingly open to discussion. The website was founded by photographer Nick Knight and graphic designer Peter Saville with the aim of redefining the boundaries of how fashion was presented online. Nick Knight describes SHOWstudio as being based on the idea that "showing the entire creative process — from conception to completion — is beneficial for the artist, the audience and the art itself."[2] According to Alexander Fury, the platform's fashion director, this notion resulted in the website's three founding principles: process, performance and participation.[3] Initially, SHOWstudio focused mainly on performance; creating stand-alone, short fashion films in collaboration with designers such as Alexander McQueen, John Galliano and Martin Margiela, and the model Kate Moss. There was, and still is, plenty of scope for experimentation. In addition to its performance-oriented films, the website soon started to provide more insight into the process, through webcasts of interviews with key figures from the fashion industry and live broadcasts from photo shoots and subsequently, starting in October 2009, live streams of catwalk shows. Nowadays, *SHOWstudio.com* also includes a webshop which enables clothing and accessories from the short films to be ordered online at the simple click of a button.

SHOWstudio co-founder Nick Knight (1958) started his career at a time when the fashion houses were just beginning to develop closer relationships with art directors, who they hoped would help them create a visual identity that would make a lasting impression on consumers. Knight joined British fashion magazine *i-D* in 1985. His portraits caught the eye of art director Marc Ascoli, and he asked Knight to handle the photography for Japanese designer Yohji Yamamoto's lookbook and advertising campaign in 1986. Knight involved graphic designer Peter Saville (1955), known for producing album sleeves for the likes of Joy Division and New Order while at Factory Records, in the project, and the trio created a series of — what would go down in fashion history as groundbreaking — images; their Yamamoto lookbooks have since become collectors' items. Saville himself refers to this collaboration as 'Year Zero': the start of his minimalistic approach in which he based his designs only on the absolute necessities. The innovative photos by Ascoli, Knight and Saville for Yohji Yamamoto — Naomi Campbell in profile wearing a red bustle, Susie Bick slumped on a chair with a cigarette between her fingers — have a tremendous impact to this day, and have been instrumental in developing the Yamamoto brand's visual identity.

The rise of the role of art directors in the Eighties, and their influence in developing visual identities for fashion labels, is covered in more detail in this book in the article by design historian Tamsin Blanchard. Blanchard points out that the fashion industry is one of the most competitive and saturated markets and that a good design is simply not enough to guarantee the success of a fashion label. A person's motivation for choosing a white T-shirt from HEMA, American Apparel, Hugo Boss or Comme des Garçons is not only a matter of budget, but also of the visual identity the label expresses. The way a fashion label communicates this identity is mainly determined by the codes it integrates into its marketing — advertisements, packaging and store design — rather than by the designs themselves.[4] These codes are the reason that a businessman is more likely to choose a Hugo Boss T-shirt while an architect will probably prefer a Comme des Garçons design. The codes that fashion labels use to communicate are not universal; different codes appeal to different worlds.

2 http://showstudio.com/studio/about.

3 http://www.premsela.org/fashion-culture/the-perfect-cut/.

4 Tamsin Blanchard, 'Fashion & Graphics: Introduction', in: Malcolm Barnard (ed.), *Fashion Theory: A Reader*, Routledge 2007, p. 535.

Catalogue for Yohji Yamamoto, photographed by Nick Knight, art direction by Marc Ascoli, A/W 1988–1989

Clockwise from top to bottom:
Catherine Deneuve in *Belle de Jour*, 1967;
John Galliano, S/S 1997; Prada, *First Spring*,
directed by Yang Fudong, S/S 2010;
Rodarte, still from *Aanteni*, directed by Todd Cole, 2010;
Rodarte, still from *The Curve of Forgotten Things*,
directed by Todd Cole, S/S 2011

A key factor in the emergence of the art director's role precisely in the mid-Eighties, rather than sooner or later, was the ever greater level of competition in the fashion industry at that time. Luxury product conglomerates such as LVMH, PPR, Gucci Group and Prada had started buying up fashion houses. LVMH in particular, was involved in a number of lavish takeovers: it acquired Givenchy, Marc Jacobs, Kenzo, Fendi and Donna Karan all in the course of the Nineties. LVMH then installed new designers, including John Galliano at Christian Dior, Alexander McQueen at Givenchy and Marc Jacobs at Louis Vuitton, to breathe new life into the fashion houses and to attract a new and younger audience, and their actions were paralleled by the other conglomerates. This period also saw the major fashion houses increasingly attempting to widen their audiences. They achieved this 'democratisation' of the luxury goods market by developing cheaper sub-labels and reducing the prices of their prestigious products.[5] This meant no longer approaching the luxury goods market from a socio-demographic point of view, but instead viewing it as a collection of 'commodified mini-milieus' which evolved based on shared style tastes. In turn, these shared tastes were founded on items of status and the need to express oneself through consumption. Each mini-milieu maintained status as its only goal, and the only difference between them was the preference for specific luxury products.[6] In order to set themselves apart from their competitors in such an ambitious market, the fashion houses required more than simply a 'good product'. They needed to develop a brand identity that would appeal to the desire of the commodified mini-milieus for status, and thus convince them to buy their products. And that's how the function of the art director came into being: from the need of the fashion houses to differentiate themselves by creating their own visual identity. With their Yohji Yamamoto Autumn/Winter campaign in 1986, Marc Ascoli, Nick Knight and Peter Saville were the first to attempt to do so, and before long the art director had become an integral part of the fashion world.

With the growth of broadband internet and social media channels such as Twitter and Facebook, visual marketing opportunities have expanded to include the creation of slick websites which allow a fashion house's ups and downs to be followed live. At shows, editors from leading fashion magazines have been supplanted from the front row by influential bloggers such as Scott Schuman from weblog *The Sartorialist*, and Garance Doré and Tommy Ton from Jak & Jil[7] who post their reviews either live or just minutes after the show has finished. Furthermore, it has become the rule rather than the exception that fashion-week catwalk shows are streamed live. Burberry, one of fashion's social media leaders, even did so in 3D, a technique that is only expected to gain in popularity in the future. Alexander McQueen's 'Plato's Atlantis' show for Summer 2010 marked the debut of Lady Gaga's new single *Bad Romance*. A live stream of the show could be followed on *SHOWstudio.com*, or at least, that was the plan. Due to an overwhelming number of viewers, the website's system became overloaded and went offline for several hours, so the images could only be viewed afterwards. In addition to live streaming, more and more fashion designers are choosing the short fashion film as the vehicle for presenting their new collection. Whereas fashion houses select big-name Hollywood directors for their perfume commercials, designers prefer to position their short fashion films, which are only broadcast on the internet and not on TV, in the grey area between film and art. American fashion label Proenza Schouler picked controversial art-house director Harmony Korine to capture its streetwise and youthful fashion on film, Prada chose young Chinese video

5 Twitchell, *Living It Up: Our Love Affair with Luxury*, Simon & Schuster 2003, p. 29.

6 Gottdiener, *New Forms of Consumption: Consumers, Culture, and Commodification*, Rowman & Littlefield Publishers 2000, p. 17. See also: Nicky Ryan, 'Prada and the Art of Patronage', in: *Fashion Theory*, Volume 11, Issue 1, Berg 2007, pp. 10–11.

7 Between them, these three bloggers generated around 320,000 hits per day in 2010.

Alexander McQueen, *Plato's Atlantis*, S/S 2010

artist Yang Fudong to reinforce its artistic image and Comme des Garçons, a fashion label renowned for its inventiveness and conceptual approach, collaborated with stop-motion animators The Quay Brothers. Each of these were carefully considered decisions aimed at supporting and strengthening the particular label's visual identity.

One pioneer of the short fashion film is British designer Gareth Pugh (1981). Ever since his A/W 2009–2010 collection, he has regularly presented his collections using films, which he has produced in collaboration with SHOW-studio.com and director Ruth Hogben. His extravagant, S&M- and gothic-inspired designs are not the only giveaway to his roots in East London's colourful club scene; his fashion films reveal them too. Under Hogben's direction and accompanied by a throbbing techno beat, androgynous models such as Natasa Vojnovic, Kirsten McMenamy and Raquel Zimmerman perform acrobatic dance moves, their distorted body shapes taking on dramatic proportions. Hogben's kaleidoscopic, almost hypnotic images perfectly complement Gareth Pugh's visual language. Characteristic of his designs are stripes, monochrome colours, billowing fabrics and balloon-like proportions — features which are all ideally suited for film. When asked about the reason for his transition from catwalk shows to films for his new collections, Pugh is unequivocal: "I really want to present my clothes to a wider audience and in a more freeing and interesting context than a standard fashion show," he explained to the *Wall Street Journal*. He also added that he regarded the fashion film as a "modern alternative" to live catwalk events, and that making a film gave him the opportunity to regain "total artistic and creative freedom."[8] In another interview, Pugh said: "It was about bringing it to a wider audience and about having complete control over what I bring to that audience. So many things can go wrong with a show and so many things can go wrong in a film but people don't see those mistakes. It was about taking back control and showing them what I want them to see."[9] More freedom, reaching a larger and wider audience, having control – these are all valid reasons to switch from catwalk shows to fashion films. Another fashion house that chooses to use film, albeit this time alongside its catwalk shows, is Mugler, which received a welcome boost in 2010 when stylist Nichola Formichetti was named as creative director. To present his first collection for Mugler (the A/W 2011–2012 menswear collection), Formichetti — a personal friend and regular stylist of Lady Gaga — enlisted the help of photographer Mariano Vivanco to make a short film. The result was a simple, black-and-white film featuring the model Rick Genest (aka Zombie Boy) whose body is literally covered with breathtaking tattoos. His head, which is tattooed as a partially open skull, is a work of graphic art in itself — its macabre beauty is simply captivating. In combination with an exclusive new track from Lady Gaga, it's no wonder this film has generated more than 1.6 million hits on YouTube. Somewhat more refined was the short film that fashion designer Issey Miyake commissioned from Mio Ueta and Masashi Sato for his A-POC label. Running for almost three minutes, the film shows a number of animated silhouettes made up of the letters that spell Issey Miyake, as well as dots, dashes and circles, all against a black background. The silhouettes change shape in time to the music, in a reference to the philosophy behind A-POC (short for 'a piece of cloth'), namely that the consumers themselves determine their garment's ultimate form by cutting into the fabric.

Not everyone is unreservedly enthusiastic about the rise of the short fashion film. Art director Marc Ascoli, mentioned above in relation to his groundbreak-

8 http://blogs.wsj.com/runway/ 2010/09/29/gareth-pugh-skips-runway- for-film/.

9 http://fashionista.com/2010/10/ jefferson-hack-interviews-gareth-pugh- about-making-fashion-films-over-runway- shows-and-his-hong-kong-store/.

Proenza Schouler, *Snowballs*, directed by Harmony Korine, 2011

ing work for Yohji Yamamoto, found the films by Martin Scorsese (for Chanel) and David Lynch (for Dior) disappointing. "It's very 'bling bling' nowadays to hire big names," Ascoli told the *Daily Tiger*, the daily publication of the International Film Festival in Rotterdam. The 2011 edition of the festival featured a side programme of lectures, including *The Perfect Cut*, examining the phenomenon of fashion films. Ascoli believes that such films add nothing to the brand. Afraid of getting left behind and in an attempt to appeal to the general public, fashion houses have switched en masse to making short fashion films, thinking that a budget big enough to hire the industry's most expensive photographers, directors, stylists and make-up artists guarantees a good film. They are sadly mistaken. Only when film-makers take their time, and take fashion seriously, can the fashion film really make a contribution to a fashion label's visual identity, is his opinion.[10] On the other hand, film-maker Zach Gold, who took part in *The Perfect Cut* with his film *String Theory* for the A.F. Vandevorst fashion label, predominantly sees opportunities. Thanks to the internet, television with its thirty-second commercial slots is no longer the fashion film's only hope of gaining exposure. Instead, there are numerous portals: *YouTube*, online platforms for fashion film, and fashion labels' websites, that can represent a podium for fashion films of any length. Rather than perusing a fifteen-page fashion spread in a magazine, we're much more likely to be watching a fifteen-minute fashion film on our iPads in the future, Gold predicts.[11]

From recent films such as *Black Swan* and *Io Sono L'Amore*, in which costumes from fashion labels like Rodarte and Jil Sander added an extra dimension to the storyline, and the stand-alone fashion films by Gareth Pugh and Rodarte, to the countless live-streamed broadcasts of catwalk shows during fashion weeks, the fashion film is here to stay — and is set to play an increasingly prominent role in the years ahead. Film appears to offer limitless possibilities. Whereas any number of things can go wrong during a catwalk show, a film allows designers to retain control and exploit a wealth of opportunities — with or without the help of an art director — to create a visual identity that can make a lasting impression on consumers among the endless stream of images that they are confronted with every day. Supported by the increasingly technologically advanced internet and its social media channels, modern-day designers have been given the chance to reclaim their freedom, and this is particularly beneficial for designers who are just starting out. You no longer need to go to a fashion city such as Paris, London, Milan or New York to launch your collection; a well-designed website and an active social-media presence can get you a long way. And so, after the first wave of democratisation brought about by the rise of the luxury conglomerates such as LVMH, PPR, Gucci Group and Prada in the Nineties, we are now seeing a second wave. And the general public is benefiting from it just as much as the fashion designers themselves, if not more so: thanks to websites such as SHOWstudio.com and Nowness.com, and portals like *YouTube* and *Vimeo*, a couple of mouse-clicks give consumers front-row seats at the major catwalk shows, a look behind the scenes on a fashion shoot with photographers such as Inez van Lamsweerde & Vinoodh Matadin, and allow them the indulgence of a five-minute fashion editorial in which Nick Knight presents the season's latest looks — complete with moving images.

10 Georgette Koning, 'The Perfect Cut: Marc Ascoli', in: *The Daily Tiger*, 5-02-2011, p. 13.

11 Mo Veld, 'Internet is de ontmoetings-plaats voor mode en cinema', in: *The Daily Tiger*, p. 13.

The website SHOWstudio.com was launched in November 2000 as a platform for fashion films and moving images. According to co-founder and owner Nick Knight, it is the ideal medium for promoting clothing in a digital age. He and his fellow co-founder Peter Saville set out to redefine the boundaries of how fashion is presented online, and the website is based on three founding principles: process, performance and participation.[1]

In its early years, SHOWstudio was primarily concerned with creating stand-alone, short fashion films working with designers such as Alexander McQueen and John Galliano and models including Kate Moss and Naomi Campbell. The website also collaborated with artists, musicians and actors such as Tracey Emin, Björk and Brad Pitt. The focus was clearly on performance, and *SHOWstudio.com* featured many experimental videos. One of the most unusual films was for the project called *Sleep*: eight models were dressed in the latest catwalk collections and had their hair and make-up done before subsequently getting into bed and going to sleep.[2] Visitors to the website could observe how the carefully-styled looks of the models gradually deteriorated as they slept. These performance-oriented films were soon followed by a growing desire to provide an insight into the process. SHOWstudio chose to do this using various webcasts, interviews with leading figures from the fashion industry, live broadcasts from photo shoots and live footage from catwalk shows. The honours for the first live-streamed fashion show went to Alexander McQueen's S/S 2010 collection in October 2009.

The webshop that opened in July 2009 has increased the high degree of audience participation on SHOWstudio even further by enabling visitors to order the clothing and accessories featured in the website's videos, films and catwalk shows with just a couple of clicks of the mouse. The products are often unique items selected by the designers themselves. Designers who have sold their designs through the SHOWstudio webshop include the likes of Gareth Pugh, Stephen Jones and Giles Deacon.

www.showstudio.com

Peter Saville & Julie Verhoeven, *Forget-Me-Not*, 2001

1 http://www.premsela.org/fashion-culture/the-perfect-cut/.
2 http://showstudio.com/project/sleep/.

Daniel Brown, Nick Knight & Liberty Ross,
still from *Dress Me Up, Dress Me Down*, 2005

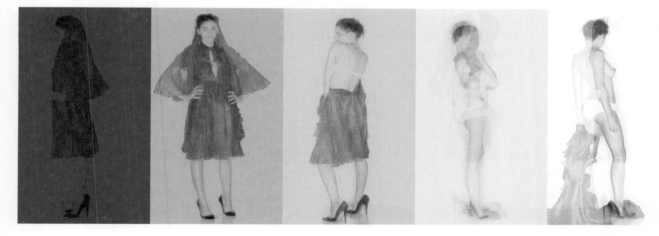

Since launching her blog 'A Shaded View On Fashion (ASVOF)' in 2005, Diane Pernet has become a leading authority on fashion. Every month, more than 160,000 readers visit her website to gain insights into the latest developments in the world of fashion in general, and the avant-garde in particular.

Having studied documentary film-making at Temple University in Philadelphia, Pernet started her career as a lo-fi film-maker. She has also worked as a fashion designer and a film-costume designer, and as a fashion editor for magazines such as *Joyce* and websites including Elle.com and Vogue.fr. Furthermore, she was a talent scout for the Hyères Festival from 2002 to 2011, and she has been co-editor in chief of *Zoo Magazine* since 2007. In September 2008, Diane Pernet held the first edition of what would become an annual film festival dedicated to fashion in Galerie Nationale du Jeu de Paume in Paris.

Sharing its name with her blog, the inaugural event of 'A Shaded View On Fashion Film (ASVOFF)' featured films, documentaries, conferences, performances and installations by the likes of Mike Figgis, Erwin Olaf, Nobuyoshi Araki, Steven Klein, Chris Cunningham, Chlöe Sevigny, Ruth Hogben and Nick Knight.

She has since organised numerous other events related to fashion and film, including ones in the Guggenheim Museum in Bilbao, the Palazzo Morando in Milan and the Barbican Art Gallery in London.

Speaking on film's influence on fashion, Diane Pernet says: "I think the 'fashion film' was born out of a real need to breathe life into the old static medium and set fashion in motion through the magic of cinema. What ASVOFF does is to give people in both industries — and talented outsiders too — a platform to let this genre flourish."[1] So convinced is she by the power of the medium, she predicts that the fashion film will eventually replace the catwalk show as a vehicle for presenting new collections — although she herself admits that it is probably still a long way off.

www.ashadedviewonfashion.com

1 http://www.huffingtonpost.co.uk/2011/10/06/diane-pernet-on-a-shade-v_n_997816.html.

Diane Pernet

Through his La Fortuna Studio, Spanish photographer and film-maker Javier Barcala (1981) has created a number of colourful and groundbreaking short fashion films in recent years. The common themes running through his work are social conscience and the striving for progress.

At the age of twenty-two, Barcala moved to Antwerp to study at the Royal Academy of Fine Arts. There, he discovered the work of Walter Van Beirendonck, Vivienne Westwood and Katharine Hamnett, and realised that fashion could be used to make a statement. Barcala: "I actually don't think there's anything frivolous about fashion, it's an integral part of our being and probably one of the most complex and interesting sources of identity. It's about showing who you are, socially, sexually and politically."[1] With this in mind, Javier Barcala spent a number of years working for H&M's Fashion Against Aids, developing the advertising campaign. Barcala then went on to channel all his energy into La Fortuna Studio. He also made two very special short fashion films for the A/W 2011–2012 and S/S 2012 collections of Belgian fashion designer Christophe Coppens. For the latter film, he enlisted the help of singer Róisín Murphy,who not only composed the soundtrack for the kaleidoscopic film but also featured in it — she can be seen as an exotic samurai warrior. For this collection, Coppens collaborated with Belgian basket-weaver Lieve Lieckens who transformed sculptural pieces of woven straw into haute couture.

In 2010, Javier Barcala and La Fortuna Studio launched a project called *The Believers: Smashing Future Fashion*. In an attempt to alter the widely held view that sustainable fashion cannot be high fashion, Barcala invited several young designers from Japan, The Netherlands, Belgium and Denmark to work together on creating this green fashion collection, for which he himself produced a series of short, promotional fashion films.

www.lafortunastudio.com

Christophe Coppens, *The Collector*, A/W 2011–2012

1 http://dianepernet.typepad.com/diane/2010/08/philippe-pourhashemi-interviews-javier-barcala.html.

Right from the start of his career, photographer Nick Knight (1958) has been constantly trying to challenge conventional thoughts on beauty. His first book *Skinheads* (1982), which Knight published while still a photography student at the Bournemouth & Poole College of Art and Design, attracted the attention of Terry Jones, founder of *i-D*, who asked him to produce one hundred portrait shots for the magazine's fifth anniversary. They caught the eye of Marc Ascoli, who selected Knight to work with him and graphic designer Peter Saville on a range of lookbooks and advertisements for Japanese fashion designer Yohji Yamamoto. The trio created a series of groundbreaking images, and Yamamoto was so impressed with the result that Knight's collaboration with him lasted for the next twelve seasons. By then, fashion magazines and labels were queuing up to hire Nick Knight. Over the years, Knight has done shoots for publications including *Vogue*, *Dazed & Confused*, *W magazine*, *Visionaire*, *Another Magazine* and *Another Man* and for advertising campaigns for labels such as Christian Dior, Alexander McQueen, Calvin Klein, Levi Strauss, Yves Saint Laurent, Lancôme and Vivienne Westwood.

"I don't want to reflect social change — I want to cause social change."[1] Nick Knight once said. Hence disability, racism, age discrimination and 'the thin ideal' are recurring themes in his photographs. Images Knight took for the September 1998 edition of the magazine *Dazed & Confused* featured para-athlete Aimee Mullins, whose legs had to be amputated when she was a year old. He was also the first photographer to capture plus-size model Sophie Dahl on film. Knight's fascination for unconventional beauty has made him popular with artists such as Björk and Lady Gaga, who — as illustrated by both their music and their appearances – clearly share his interest in the topic. He regularly works with Lady Gaga for the website *SHOWstudio.com*, the platform for fashion films that he co-launched in 2000.

www.nickknight.com

1 http://www.vogue.co.uk/spy/biographies/nick-knight-biography.

Nick Knight, Alexander McQueen & Michael Clark, still from *Mac III*, 2004

Film-maker Ruth Hogben began her career under photographer Nick Knight's wings, working as his assistant from 2005 to 2009 — initially on photographic projects, and later on film projects too. Hogben made her first film in 2007; after fooling around with a video camera while accompanying Knight on a fashion shoot for *Arena Homme +*, she edited the material into a thirty-second film for *SHOWstudio.com*. When she did the same during a shoot for a *Dazed & Confused* issue that was focusing on young British designer Gareth Pugh and his A/W 2008–2009 collection, she found it so inspiring that she decided to concentrate on making short fashion films full-time.

Over the years, Ruth Hogben has developed particularly strong ties with Gareth Pugh. For his A/W 2009–2010 collection, Pugh opted to present his latest designs in a short fashion film rather than a catwalk show, and this marked Hogben's first produc-tion as an independent film-maker. She regards Pugh's extravagant designs, inspired by S&M and Gothicism, as ideally suited to the medium of film, and she enjoys the challenge of bringing the details and textures to life. Rather than working with a narrative, Hogben approaches the short fashion film as a dynamic photo-graph in which clothing and movement are the key elements. One common element in all her short fashion films are forceful, assertive women. For her, it is not about their sexuality — as is so often the case in fashion films and photographs — but about their strength and intelligence. A prime example of this was her collaboration with pop star Lady Gaga: together with Nick Knight, Hogben created a series of short films which were shown as intermezzos in Gaga's *Monster Ball* Tour, which ran from 2009 to 2011.

www.ruthhogben.com

Lady Gaga, still from *Bone Tattoo*, directed by Nick Knight and Ruth Hogben, 2011

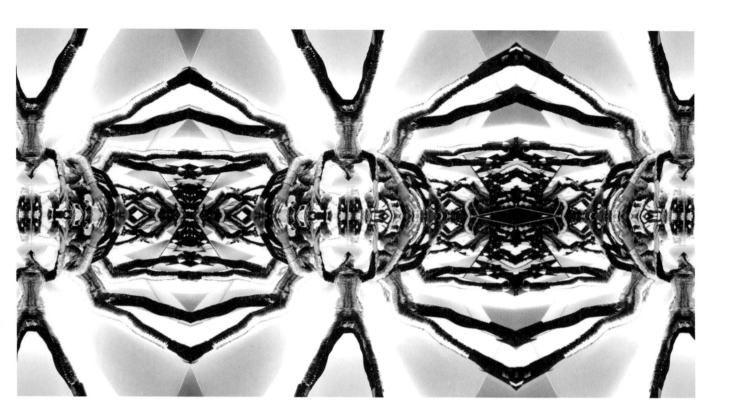

Top: Gareth Pugh, still from a film by Ruth Hogben, A/W 2011–2012
Bottom: Gareth Pugh, still from a film by Ruth Hogben, S/S 2011

Top: Lady Gaga, still from the music video *Alejandro*, directed Steven Klein, 2010
Bottomr: Lady Gaga, still from the music video *Born This Way*, directed by Nick Knight, 2011

Not since the emergence of Madonna in the late Eighties has a pop star caused such a stir as Lady Gaga (1986). Gaga, real name Stefani Germanotta, became involved in music at an early age. Her breakthrough came in 2008 with the release of her first album *The Fame*, which included chart hits such as *Poker Face* and *Paparazzi*. It was followed by albums *The Fame Monster*, which featured the singles *Bad Romance*, *Alejandro* and *Telephone*, in 2009 and *Born This Way* in 2011.

Lady Gaga's look is just as important as her music, if not more so. Her early performances were influenced by the styles of burlesque and go-go dancing. By the time her first album was released, Lady Gaga had assembled her own group of creative people around her who collectively called themselves 'Haus of Gaga'. Modelled on Andy Warhol's 'The Factory', members of the Haus of Gaga make many of her costumes and decors. Since May 2009, Gaga has been working with stylist Nicola Formichetti, who creates her looks for performances, videos and other personal appearances. The general rule of thumb seems to be: 'the wilder, the better'. For both her wardrobe and, in a broader sense, the overall Gaga performance, sources of inspiration for Formichetti and Lady Gaga include the eccentric performance artist Leigh Bowery, the S&M culture and pop stars such as Madonna, Cher, David Bowie and legendary Queen frontman, Freddie Mercury.

Similar influences are also clear in her extravagant music videos. Gaga herself prefers to regard them as short films which enable her to tell a story, and she often works with people from the world of fashion. For example, Nick Knight directed the video for Gaga's single *Born This Way*, and he collaborated with Ruth

Lady Gaga, photographed by Hedi Slimane, 2009

Hogben to produce a number of visuals for her *Monster Ball* tour. Fashion photographers Inez van Lamsweerde & Vinoodh Matadin created a series of short videos based on Gaga's character from her single *Yoü and I*. She also supports SHOWstudio.com, and even took part in a two-hour-long live interview in May 2010. The website also regularly features new and exclusive material from her, such as music videos and short films.

www.ladygaga.com

Lady Gaga, still from the music video *Telephone*, directed by Jonas Åkerlund, 2010

FASHION, TECHNOLOGY & THE SMARTPHONE

— HANKA VAN DER VOET & JOSÉ TEUNISSEN

Forward thinking is a term that characterises the fashion world well, both literally in terms of the collections that are presented earlier and earlier every year, with the catwalks now happy to show us what we will be wearing a year from now, as well as figuratively with increasing numbers of fashion designers experimenting with new materials and techniques in order to demonstrate what they feel the ideal fashions for the future should be. For a brief moment at the start of the twenty-first century, it seemed that fashion was on the verge of a major transformation. Electronics company Philips and other household names were experimenting with integrating electronic devices into clothing, but both the technology (the wires tended to break) and the designs were a disappointment. The prototypes failed during testing and never made it into the fashion industry as a whole. However, such technological innovations did attract attention from sports and outdoor clothing brands such as Nike, Adidas, Speedo and North Face, organisations which continued investigating the capabilities of the latest fibres and 'intelligent' fabrics: moisture wicking, conductive, UV protective, on a large scale, producing innovative sportswear that delivers better performance and greater comfort.

In fashion, the primary consideration is a garment's aesthetics and the message it communicates rather than its function or comfort. Anne Hollander describes "dress as a form of visual art with the visible self as its medium."[1] Our choice of fashion/clothing gives us our individual and social identities: the outside world can see who we are and to which social group we belong. Yet this role is potentially set to diminish. Now that almost everyone on the streets is wandering around with their eyes fixed firmly on their smartphone, the concept of 'seeing and being seen' in public is losing its significance and is being replaced by the importance of a 'virtual' identity through channels such as Twitter, Facebook and other social media. It therefore will not be long before fashion undergoes a noticeable transformation. After all, what is fashion going to look like if people are expressing their identities predominantly in a virtual world while paying little attention to what there is to see around them? In recent years, a handful of innovative designers such as Hussein Chalayan, Issey Miyake and Helen Storey have been freely experimenting. Issey Miyake

1 Anne Hollander, *Seeing through Clothes*, Avedon, New York 1975, p. 9.

is known for relentless curiosity and desire to preserve traditional handcrafts using modern technology and fabrics. He and Helen Storey have explored the different relationships between the body, clothes and the world at large. Now that new, bio-based fabrics made from celluloses and enzymes are available, along with technology such as 3D printers and all manner of digital design tools, not only will fashion look different, but it will also be produced using completely different processes. Fashion history is already in motion, but how exactly did we get here?

DESIGNING THE FUTURE

Forward thinking is not only a recurring theme in fashion, it also echoes through cinema, fine art and literature. Especially in times of significant progress, such as the industrial revolution in the nineteenth century, after the first moon landing in 1969, the growth of the personal computer in the Eighties and current developments around biotechnology and robotics; the arts reflected on these changes, the chances they presented and the problems associated with them. Science-fiction pioneers such as Jules Verne and H.G. Wells let their imaginations run wild in their groundbreaking novels *20,000 Leagues Under the Sea* (1870) and *The War of the Worlds* (1898), when their heads were full of all the technological opportunities opened up by the industrial revolution.

The 1960s saw a veritable explosion in science-fiction writing and films. NASA's Apollo space programme and its attempt to land a man on the moon captivated millions of people all over the world. In fact this period seemed to offer endless possibilities, but not all of them positive. The world was gripped by the Cold War which subsequently escalated into an arms race between the USA and the Soviet Union, and the threat of nuclear war was never far away — a situation which inspired Stanley Kubrick to direct his satirical film *Dr. Strangelove* in 1964. His subsequent film, *2001: A Space Odyssey* (1968) which examined the topic of intelligence in humans, animals and technology, also reflected what was on people's minds at that time.

1968 also saw the release of Roger Vadim's film *Barbarella* starring Jane Fonda in the leading role. This tongue-in-cheek film tells the story of the character Barbarella, who is sent from outer space to save the Earth. The film's costumes were designed by the Spanish designer Paco Rabanne (1934), who launched his own fashion house in 1966 after having worked for Balenciaga, Christian Dior and Givenchy. By using unconventional materials like metal, paper and plastic in his designs, former architect Rabanne was soon labelled an 'enfant terrible', but he can lay claim to being one of the first to take a futuristic, technological approach to fashion design. Just a few years earlier, in 1964, the French designer (and qualified engineer) André Courrèges had introduced his *Space Age* collection which was constructed entirely around geometric shapes and featured materials such as PVC and metal. Courrèges and Rabanne were the first to try to give fashion and clothing a new look using new materials and techniques. Yet while the collections attracted a huge amount of media attention, the designs were too outlandish to become a commercial success.

NEW DESIGN AND CONSTRUCTION PROCESSES

2 Valerie Steele, *Japan Fashion Now*, Yale University Press, New Haven 2010, p. 19.

3 Barbara Vinken, *Fashion Zeitgeist: Trends and Cycles in the Fashion System*, Berg Publishers, Oxford 2004.

More recently, it has been mainly Japanese fashion designers who have been experimenting with new, technologically advanced materials. Anyone studying the work of the likes of Rei Kawakubo from Comme des Garçons, Yohji Yamamoto, Issey Miyake and Junya Watanabe will conclude that they all use materials as the starting point for their design processes. These designers often employ experts or even have their own laboratories to enable them to create new fabrics. Kawakubo and Yamamoto presented their clothes on the Paris catwalks for the first time in 1981 at a time when Japan's economy was booming and the country was at the forefront of the technological and imminent digital revolution. Draped loosely over the body, asymmetrical and predominantly black, the garments from Rei Kawakubo's Comme des Garçons and Yohji Yamamoto caused a huge stir due to the radically avant-garde nature of the designs, which fashion journalists described as 'rags' and 'holocaust chic'.[2] In her book *Fashion Zeitgeist* (2004), Barbara Vinken calls Rei Kawakubo and Yohji Yamamoto's designs "post-fashion" and claims that their arrival in Paris signified the start of a new era which would bring an end to the 'fashion of a hundred years'; fashion by the likes of Charles F. Worth and Yves Saint Laurent.[3]

Junya Watanabe, S/S 2000

Some Japanese designers were much more concerned with the 'image', the 'concept' and the 'experience' than with the garments themselves. What has set Issey Miyake apart from his contemporaries has not only been a desire to preserve traditional handcrafts using modern technology; but also a relentless drive to find new ways of making things, independent of the world of fashion or haute couture. Launched in 1993, PLEATS PLEASE ISSEY MIYAKE was the culmination of Miyake's quest for clothing as universal as jeans and T-shirts. As he evolved further, A-POC (an acronym for 'A Piece of Cloth') introduced in 1998, took Miyake's themes of making clothing from one piece of cloth to a new level. The A-POC technique wed first an industrial knitting then later a weaving machine to computer technology that created fabric, texture and fully-finished garments in a single process. His most recent evolution of A Piece of Cloth, called 132 5. ISSEY MIYAKE, generates 3D shapes on a sheet of paper using a computer. These are then reproduced in recycled PET polyester using the basic principles of origami. Thus, the normal design and production cycle of choosing the fabric, making sketches and a pattern, and then sewing it all together, has been eliminated. Once again, Miyake is working with a modern process to create clothing as a product that also fulfils the needs of a modern lifestyle.

Junya Watanabe, S/S 2003

A DIFFERENT TAKE ON BODY, SHAPE, SPACE AND SURROUNDINGS

The younger generation of Japanese fashion designers has also displayed an interest in the opportunities presented by new technology. Junya Watanabe (1961) achieved fame as Rei Kawakubo's protégé. After graduating from the Bunka Fashion College in Tokyo, he began his career at Comme des Garçons in 1984 and was allowed to develop his own line for the label in 1992. Just like those of his mentor Kawakubo, Watanabe's designs challenge boundaries and toy with the conventions associated with shape, body and movement. Similarly, his collections have been hailed 'techno couture' due to his application of innovative materials.

Watanabe launched his first techno-couture collection in 1996: futuristic, colourful designs made from cellophane. His fascination with innovation mainly benefits the functionality of his clothing, like in his Autumn/Winter 1999–2000 collection, for example, when he designed jackets that could be folded up to create bags. His Summer 2000 collection, *Function and Practicality*, included several waterproof garments including evening gowns. Clothes made from 'intelligent' fabrics had previously looked more like military uniforms than everyday outfits, whereas Watanabe's *Function and Practicality* collection demonstrated just how versatile these fabrics were. And while the title might have seemed to lack inspiration, Junya Watanabe's *Function and Practicality* collection included attractive and elegant dresses that the models wore while walking down the catwalk through a simulated shower of rain.

A generation further down the line, fashion designer Hussein Chalayan (1970) has been making an impression with his technologically advanced creations. Chalayan was born in the Turkish community of Northern Cyprus, but moved with his family to the UK in 1978. Chalayan graduated from the Central Saint Martins College of Art and Design in 1993 with his collection called *The Tangent Flows*, which included garments that he had sprinkled with iron filings and buried in the garden only to exhume them to see how they had decomposed. Hussein Chalayan was different from the other fashion students at Saint Martins. He rarely read fashion magazines; he preferred books on philosophy and history, and was more interested in notions than in clothing. His technical skill and his talent for translating his ideas on nature, culture and technology into a coherent collection came to a climax in three successive collections in 1999 and 2000. In collaboration with industrial designer Paul Topen, Hussein Chalayan — who as a young boy had dreamed of becoming a pilot — produced three dresses by pouring fibre glass and resin into a mould, a technique used in the aerospace industry. The first collection to feature a dress from this project was *Geotropics* in the summer of 1999. It was like a chair that you carried with you all the time, with a headrest, armrests and a seat. The model presenting the dress on the catwalk wore little else other than nude-coloured underwear and a bandage around her head: the designer's reference to the nakedness and vulnerability of humankind. By contrasting this with the rigid technology of the material and the construction techniques from the aerospace industry, Chalayan wanted to highlight the difference between the inorganic and the organic. He had created a kind of cyborg: half human, half machine.[4]

The two dresses that followed went even further in their uses of innovative and unconventional materials and techniques. They were supplied with remote controls that made sections of the dress move up and down like an aeroplane's flaps when preparing to land. Bradley Quinn, author of *Techno Fashion* (2003), describes the 'aeroplane dresses' as technologised sexualisation of the body. The panels open to reveal erogenous zones and manipulate the body to conform to the ideals of sex appeal.[5] Quinn commends Chalayan for his ability to integrate the world around him into his designs by creating something that is a reflection of the environment that shapes it. Hussein Chalayan himself commented: "Everything around us either relates to the body or to the environ-

4 Caroline Evans, *Fashion at the Edge: Spectacle, Modernity, and Deathliness*, Yale University Press, New Haven 2007, p. 274.

5 Bradley Quinn, *Techno Fashion*, Berg Publishers, Oxford 2002, p. 51.

6 Bradley Quinn, 'A Note: Hussein Chalayan, Fashion and Technology', in: *Fashion Theory*, Volume 6, Issue 4, Berg Publishers, Oxford 2002, p. 362.

Hussein Chalayan, *The Tangent Flows*, 1993

Hussein Chalayan, *Geotropics*, S/S 1999

Clockwise from top to bottom:
Helen Storey, *Wonderland*, 2008;
Iris van Herpen, *Escapism*, S/S 2011

ment. I think of modular systems where clothes are like small parts of an interior, the interiors are part of architecture, which is then a part of an urban environment. I think of fluid space where they are all apart of each other, just in different scales and proportions."[6] What makes Chalayan's work so unique is that he explores how fashion/clothing and the body interact with the environment and their relationships with architecture or, in this case, an aeroplane.

NEW ERA, NEW TECHNOLOGIES

The past decade has seen plenty of experimentation in the field of fashion and technology, particularly in London at the University of the Arts. Suzanne Lee, for example, a professor affiliated with Central Saint Martins, enlisted the help of a chemist to develop 'BioCouture': a fabric that feels like a cross between parchment and leather made from the layer of cellulose produced in a certain kind of tea. Professor Helen Storey from London's College of Fashion collaborated with the University of Sheffield to produce the 'Disappearing dress series 2010': handmade dresses made from an enzyme-based material that slowly dissolved in water.

In this context, one designer who really stands out is Dutch designer Iris van Herpen (1984). In her sculptural designs, she combines highly refined handwork techniques such as leathercraft and modelling metal gauze, with innovative techniques such as rapid prototyping. The results have both an organic and a futuristic feel. Van Herpen's aim is to fuse the fashion of the past with the fashion of the future to create something entirely new. Three seasons ago, Iris van Herpen – who was offered but refused the chance to become creative director of fashion house Paco Rabanne in 2011 — was admitted to the French Chambre Syndicale de la Haute Couture (Trade Union of High Fashion) and she is also on the official Parisian couture calendar. What makes her work so special is the position she has managed to create for it in the official fashion world, making it accessible to a wider audience.

For her Spring/Summer 2011 collection entitled *Crystallization*, Van Herpen worked in cooperation with Benthem Crouwel Architects on several dresses made from a material called PETG, a glass-like material that crystallises when cooled slowly. The dresses looked as if they were made of solid water droplets that cascaded over the wearer. This particular collection also included Van Herpen's first piece that she designed in collaboration with architect Daniel Widrig using a 3D printer, which was a harness-like top made from a white polyamide. The top's pointy, repeated design creates the sense of the bone structure of an alien creature. While this is very impressive, it also exposes Iris van Herpen's weakness, namely that her work sometimes lacks conceptual depth and a narrative about the relationship between design and body — the essence of fashion. Her creations stand alone and do not need a body. Nevertheless, her penchant for developing three-dimensional geometric shapes around the body could put her in line as the digital successor to Walter Van Beirendonck or Henrik Vibskov.

6 Bradley Quinn, 'A Note: Hussein Chalayan, Fashion and Technology', in: *Fashion Theory*, Volume 6, Issue 4, Berg Publishers, Oxford 2002, p. 362.

Pauline van Dongen, *Kinetic Landscapes*, S/S 2012

HEADING TOWARDS A NEW RELATIONSHIP BETWEEN BODY, CLOTHING AND SPACE

Just like Iris van Herpen, Pauline van Dongen (1986) studied at the ArtEZ Institute of the Arts from where she gained her ArtEZ Fashion Masters in 2010. Van Dongen worked as an intern for Hussein Chalayan and shares his fascination for the relationship between human bodies and their environments, and the space in between. As she herself says: "I am fascinated by the interaction between people and their surroundings, body versus space and the order and arrangement of things around me. My work focuses on the surface, with fabric as a starting point. My work explores the void between the body and the garment. Different materials like synthetic crin and buntal emphasise this space. Alienating shapes or capsules floating around the body are turned into clothes, like organic sculptures." Although Van Dongen's designs are highly complex technical accomplishments, she starts the design process by moulding the materials onto the body and studying the effect that the chosen fabric has on it. Yet it is the body that always determines the shape of Van Dongen's designs rather than vice versa, as is the case with Iris van Herpen. The innovative structures contained in Pauline van Dongen's designs consistently follow the contours of the body, as seen in the laser-cut leather and silk she used in her Autumn/Winter 2011–2012 collection *Stereopsis*, and her Spring/Summer 2012 collection *Kinetic Landscapes*.

CYBER DESIGNS: NEW DIGITAL AND INTERACTIVE DESIGN TOOLS

The opportunities for technologically advanced fashion go beyond merely working with new materials and using new techniques in the production process. As A-POC (Issey Miyake and Dai Fujiwara) and 132 5. ISSEY MIYAKE projects demonstrated, fashion designers are increasingly looking to technology for assistance with the basics of the design process, i.e. drawing and sketching the designs. British designer, techie and artist Simon Thorogood has created software for various interactive design tools to help fashion designers discover fresh, innovative perspectives, such as *Planar*: a software that enables designers to apply shapes and techniques from the field of aerospace in a new context by placing them on a virtual body. And thanks to his *Sound-Wear* software, designers can translate the sonic characteristics of music into unique visualisations by connecting them to a library of shapes, colours and images which can then be projected onto the body.

FASHION AS AN EXPERIENCE OF SPACE AND BODY

As Bradley Quinn also outlines in his article, 'A Note: Hussein Chalayan, Fashion and Technology', our view of the body has traditionally been predominantly defined by social values, but the wealth of technological innovations currently emerging are having a growing impact on our attitudes towards the body. Issey Miyake, Junya Watanabe, Hussein Chalayan, Iris van Herpen and Pauline van Dongen, as well as more abstract designers such as Simon Thorogood, are using new technologies and materials to explore the physical

Left: Simon Thorogood, *SoundWear*, 2011. Right: Pauline van Dongen, *Stereopsis*, A/W 2011–2012

and psychological relationships we humans have with the world around us. Their fascination for materials and techniques results in new shapes. They use the body as a vehicle for presenting their ideas to the public about the future, corporality and sexuality, and all those elusive notions associated with it. For such designers, fashion is no longer merely about communicating one's identity. Instead, one's body and what one wears have become ideal vehicles for challenging how we regard the body and its interaction with space, with time, and if necessary, with the virtual world that is becoming such an increasingly important part of our everyday lives.

British designer and artist Simon Thorogood uses his work to explore new ways of creating and communicating fashion. He calls it *Phashion*, which is an amalgamation of the scientific term 'phase transition' with fashion, reflecting his aim to transform various ideas about fashion from a variety of sources. Simon Thorogood's 'Phashion' projects involve a certain degree of interactivity and they encourage consumers to play a role in shaping a fashion product or experience, thus enabling Thorogood to study public reactions to new ideas. He hopes that this technique of *innovention*, a cross between 'innovation' and an 'event', will lead to him developing new, creative methods within the design process. His most recent research projects have been focused on the role of originality within the traditional design process, and he has been investigating the use of simple digital systems to produce a design.

In 2008, Simon Thorogood was commissioned by the Institute of Contemporary Art (ICA) to develop *Planar*, an interactive installation and design tool which can also be used online and through an app for smartphones and tablets. This interactive design tool is based on a catalogue of shapes and techniques from the aerospace industry which users can re-contextualise by projecting them onto a virtual body. With this project, and in fact with all his recent technology-related fashion projects, Simon Thorogood endeavours to show how an atypical approach to the design process can complement a more conventional manner of designing and communicating fashion.

Another unique project is *Texturel*, an interactive, text-based design app with an 'oracle' function. If designers hit a creative block in their design process, they can ask *Texturel* for advice. The app generates a series of text-based instructions that can be interpreted in a multitude of ways. The obscure nature of the instructions could then lead to unconventional or surprising designs.

One of Thorogood's most recent projects is *SoundWear*, an interactive music-to-fashion design tool and installation. *SoundWear* works by linking certain sonic characteristics of music, such as amplitude or volume, to a digital library containing shapes, colours and images. This transforms pieces of music into personal visualisations that change in line with the sound. The *SoundWear* literally determines what music looks like.

Simon Thorogood is currently affiliated to the London College of Fashion as a Senior Research Fellow and he is a member of Fashion Digital Studio, a research centre for technology and innovation in fashion.

www.simonthorogood.com

Simon Thorogood, *SoundWear*, 2011

PLEATS
PLEASE

ISSEY MIYAKE

1994 SPRING/SUMMER

Top: ISSEY MIYAKE, PLEATS PLEASE catalogue, S/S 2004
Bottom: A-POC, *Le Feu*, 1998. ISSEY MIYAKE Paris collection, S/S 1999

Over the years, the Japanese fashion label ISSEY MIYAKE has been a pioneer in the fashion world in more ways than one. In the 1970s, it was the first Japanese label to take part in the Paris fashion week, and in 1982 Issey Miyake's designs became the first clothing to grace the cover of an art magazine (*Artforum*), thus playing a vital part in breaking down the barriers between fashion and art. Furthermore, Issey Miyake was also one of the first designers to focus on the research and development of new materials using new technologies.

Issey Miyake (1938) launched his eponymous fashion label in the early Seventies. After obtaining a degree in graphic design from the Tama Art University in Tokyo, he spent some time working in Paris and New York. In 1970 he returned to Tokyo to start his own label. Miyake is particularly famous for his PLEATS PLEASE ISSEY MIYAKE line, which made its debut in 1993. He created a wide range of pleated clothing using a specially developed polyester and his patented process of 'garment pleating' in which the garment is first cut and sewn and then put through a heat press, sandwiched between layers of paper, resulting in permanent pleats.

In 1998, Miyake teamed up with his design partner Dai Fujiwara (Design Engineer for A-POC, Creative Director for ISSEY MIYAKE, 2006–2011) to introduce a new line of clothing, choosing an acronym for his touchstone as its name: A-POC, short for 'A Piece of Cloth'. A-POC represented a new, industrial approach to design, in which the computer played a key role. Each A-POC garment was sold as a singular, tube-shaped piece of fabric. The consumer became the final piece of the process, able to extrude the item of clothing and even tailor it by cutting along the dotted lines, in effect creating a three-dimensional garment from a one-dimensional plane.

The same principle can be seen in Miyake's most recent line, '132 5. ISSEY MIYAKE', which was launched in 2010. Designed using a mathematical program based on geometric origami-like shapes, '132 5. ISSEY MIYAKE' was developed in Miyake's Reality Lab, aided by computer scientist Jun Mitani. It marks the first clothing range to be made by a computer program generating 3D shapes from a simple sheet of paper. The shapes were then reproduced by Miyake and his team, using recycled PET polyester. They proceeded to investigate how the garments could be folded up into flat, geometric shapes. When they are unfolded, they become graceful three-dimensional garments that can be worn in a variety of ways, including as a T-shirt, skirt, dress or jacket. The name '132 5. ISSEY MIYAKE' is a direct reference to this transformation: the number 1 indicates the single piece of fabric required to create a garment, the number 3 stands for the three-dimensional shape, and the number 2 refers to the fact that the design can be folded up into a two-dimensional object. The space between the 2 and the 5 represents the period of time between the folded shape being completed and the moment that someone else unfolds it into a garment and puts it on, while the 5 refers to the design's ability to take on different forms.

For the Autumn/Winter 2010–2011 collection *Mineral Miracle*, ISSEY MIYAKE's new head of design Yoshiyuki Miyamae and the technology lab developed a new textile called 'Steam Stretch'. The collection included several dresses made from a combination of silk and a stretch fabric. The team discovered that when a steam iron was applied, the stretch fabric shrank in that area, resulting in a new texture and a softer outline. The same collection also featured the use of the 'Diamond Cut' technique. It is based upon the same principals as the A-POC method, but yields a very special fabric. The material is achieved by two fine, lightweight fabrics being interwoven to create a graphic print inspired by the crystallisation of quartz.

www.isseymiyake.com

INDEX

The bold page numbers refer to images.

199

COLOPHON

This publication was made possible with the financial support of the Prins Bernhard Cultuurfonds.

© 2013 Uitgeverij Terra Lannoo bv
and authors
Terra is part of Uitgeverij Terra Lannoo bv
P.O. Box 97
3990 DB Houten
the Netherlands
info@terralannoo.nl
www.terralannoo.nl

MOTI

MOTI, Museum of the Image
Boschstraat 22
4811 GH Breda
www.motimuseum.com

ArtEZ Modelectoraat,
a department of ArtEZ Institute of the Arts
www.modelectoraat.nl

ISBN 978 90 8989 556 1
NUR 452

This book is also available in Dutch
(ISBN 978 90 8989 555 4).

Graphic design: Paul Boudens
Editors: José Teunissen, Hanka van der Voet
and Jan Brand
Image editing: Hanka van der Voet and Jan
Brand in collaboration with Andrea Kristić
Copy editing and coordination: Annelies ter
Brugge and Jan Brand
Proof-reading: Nicoline Meutstege
Translation Dutch-English: Lynn Radford,
Englishproof

Case authors:
Jos Arts: Futurism
Andrea Kristić: Raf Simons
Marij Rynja: Antoine Peters, Bernhard
Willhelm, Chanel, Katharine Hamnett,
Keith Haring, Leigh Bowery, Louis Vuitton,
Paul Smith, Sonia Delaunay, Viktor & Rolf,
Vivienne Westwood, Walter Van Beirendonck
Hanka van der Voet: A.F. Vandevorst, Alan
Aboud, BAPE, Bas Kosters, Burberry, Diane
Pernet, Dries Van Noten, Fabien Baron,
Freudenthal/Verhagen, Henrik Vibskov,
Issey Miyake, Javier Barcala, KAWS, Lady
Gaga, M/M (Paris), Mads Nørgaard, Marc
Ascoli, Maison Martin Margiela, Mevis & Van
Deursen, Nick Knight, Pascal Roulin/A-POC,
Paul Boudens, Peter Saville, Piet Parra, Ruth
Hogben, SHOWstudio, Simon Thorogood

Credits for featured articles:
Jos Arts: Clothing & Futurism. Translated
article from: Jan Brand & José Teunissen
(Eds), *Fashion and Imagination: About clothes
and art.* ArtEZ Press, d'jonge Hond 2009,
pp. 220–225.
Tamsin Blanchard: Fashion & Graphic Design.
This text is a shortened version of an essay
that was published in Malcolm Barnard (Ed.),
Fashion Theory. A Reader. Routledge 2007,
pp. 534–545

Photography credits:
Front cover: Katharine Hamnett's *Project
Ocean* for the British department store
Selfridges, 2011. Photographer unknown.
Back cover: Freudenthal/Verhagen, David
Sims & KAWS, Ronald Stoops, Dan Lecca,
Inez van Lamsweerde & Vinoodh Matadin
and M/M (Paris), Nick Knight, Ronald Stoops
Interior: Jonas Åkerlund: p. 181 (below);
Javier Barcala: p. 174, p. 175; By 2 Photog-
raphers: p. 162; Todd Cole: p. 168 (left be-
low); Pierre Debusschere: p. 42; Marc Deur-
loo: p. 145, p. 146, p. 157 (above); Charles
Dolfi-Michels © Keith Haring artwork
© Estate of Keith Haring. Image courtesy
Tate Modern: p. 116 (above); Firstview: p. 163
(above); Jean François: p. 187; Freudenthal/
Verhagen: p. 81, p. 82, p. 83, p. 132, p. 133,
p. 135, p. 154, p. 155; Yang Fudong: p. 168
(middle); Shoji Fujii: p. 149; Noam Griegst:
p. 139; Jacques Habbah: p. 65; Frederik
Heyman: p. 148 (below); Ruth Hogben: p. 178,
p. 179; Hiroshi Iwasaki: p. 186; Steven Klein:
p. 180 (above); Nick Knight: p. 58, p. 62, p. 94,
p. 95, p. 167, p. 172 (below), p. 176, p. 177,
p. 178, p. 180 (below); Barbara Kruger. Image
courtesy Mary Boone Gallery: p. 101 (above);
Karl Lagerfeld: p. 29 (left above); Inez van
Lamsweerde & Vinoodh Matadin: p. 49,
p. 52 (below), p. 54 (below), p. 55, p. 76, p. 77;
Gunnar Larsen: p. 185; Dan Lecca: p. 150,
p. 151, p. 153; Veronica Manlow: p. 164;
Craig McDean: p. 92; Ryan McGinley: p. 52
(middle); Steven Meisel: p. 47 (middle);
Mert & Marcus: p. 52 (above), p. 73; Chris
Moore. Image courtesy Hussein Chalayan:
p. 14, p. 189 (right); Mike Nicolaassen: p. 182,
p. 191, p. 193; Hordur Ellert Olafsson: p. 148
(above); Terry Richardson: p. 122; Pascal
Roulin: p. 78, p. 79; Paolo Roversi: p. 93;
Marij Rynja: p. 116 (below), p. 117; Peter
Saville & Julie Verhoeven: p. 172 (above);
SHOWstudio.com: p. 164; David Sims &
KAWS: p. 113; David Sims: p. 123; Hedi
Slimane: p. 181 (above); Patrice Stable:
p. 168 (right above); Peter Stigter: p. 16,
p. 19, p. 24, p. 29 (right above, right below),
p. 38 (below), p. 39; Ronald Stoops: p. 15,
p. 32 (below) p. 51, p. 130; Juergen Teller:
p. 126; Mario Testino: p. 23, p. 30 (right
above, left above, right below); Simon
Thorogood: p. 192, p. 194, p. 195; Willy
Vanderperre: p. 43 (below); Miguel Villalobos:
p. 173; Yasuaki Yoshinaga: p. 196 (below);
Michel Zoeter: p. 190 (right above, right
below).

With thanks to ArtEZ Fashion Masters'
students:
Stéphanie Baechler, Eline de Boer, Anna
Bornhold, Martine Bovee, Mirjam Colombo,
Ellis Droog, Lilian Heinis, Kristina Karlsson,
Barbara Langendijk, Sarah Meers, Simeon
Morris, Noon Passama, Sarah Pellis, Laura
Posdziech, Paulien Routs, Dieuwertje van
Schadewijk, Laura de Weijer, Hilda Wijnhoud
and Summer Yeh.